AUTHOR HILL, J.	CLASS E02
TITLE Nelson	

TOWN AND CITY HISTORIES
SERIES EDITOR: STEPHEN CONSTANTINE

Nelson

Politics, Economy, Community

Jeffrey Hill

KEELEUNIVERSITY**PRESS**

For Mary, Richard, Tim and Katharine

© Jeffrey Hill, 1997

Keele University Press
22 George Square, Edinburgh

Typeset in Janson Text and originated
by Carnegie Publishing Ltd, Lancaster
Printed and bound in Great Britain
by Cromwell Press, Melksham

A CIP record for this book is available
from the British Library

ISBN 1 85331 216 9

The right of Jeffrey Hill to be identified as the author
of this work has been asserted in accordance
with The Copyright, Designs and Patent Act (1988).

Contents

Series Editor's Foreword

The books in this series are designed and written with a broad readership in mind: local people interested to know how the character of their town has been shaped by major historical forces and the energies of their predecessors; newcomers and visitors curious to acquire a historical introduction to their new surroundings; general readers wishing to see how the sweeps of national and international history have manifested themselves in particular urban communities; and the scholar seeking to understand urbanisation by comparing and contrasting local experiences.

We live, most of us, in intensely urban environments. These are the products largely of the last two centuries of historical development, although the roots of many towns, of course, go back deep into the past. In recent years there has been considerable historical research of a high standard into this urban history. Narrative and descriptive accounts of the history of towns and cities can now be replaced by studies such as the TOWN AND CITY HISTORIES which investigate, analyse and, above all, explain the economic, political, social and cultural processes and consequences of urbanisation.

Writers for this series consider the changing economic foundations of their town or city and the way change has affected its physical shape, built environment, employment opportunities and urban character. The nature and interests of those who wielded power locally and the structure and functions of local government in different periods are also examined, since locally exercised authority could determine much about the fortunes and quality of urban life. Particular emphasis is placed on the changing life experiences of ordinary men, women and children – their homes, education, occupations, social relations, living standards and leisure activities. Towns and cities control and respond to the values, aspirations and actions of their residents. The books in this series therefore explore social behaviour as well as the economic and political history of those who lived in and helped make the towns and cities of today.

Stephen Constantine
University of Lancaster

Acknowledgements

I am indebted to the people who have helped in the making of this book. Most of them are people I do not, and never will, know: the many historians whose work I have drawn on, the librarians and archivists who have made material available to me, the publishers, proofreaders and printers who have actually put the book together. Without this small army of support, little would have been achieved. Their role in the production process makes me think that there can no more be an *auteur* theory of books than there can of films.

In particular, I should like to single out for thanks the staffs of the British Library, especially its newspaper branch at Colindale, the Lancashire County Record Office at Preston, the Nottingham Trent University Library, the Nottingham University Library and the Divisional Librarian and staff of the Lancashire County Council. In particular, two librarians of the Lancashire team deserve my special acknowledgements. They have been especially kind and unfailingly helpful: they are Mrs Byrne and Mrs Carradice of Nelson Public Library, who have dealt patiently and precisely with all my enquiries and put me on the right track when I have not known where to go for information. I should also like to thank Ruth and Eddie Frow of the Working Class Movement Library in Salford for allowing me to have access to files of the *Nelson Gazette*. To my own University, Nottingham Trent, I owe thanks for grants of financial assistance and study leave which enabled me to carry out some of the research upon which this book is based. Linda Dawes skilfully fashioned the maps and figures from my basic bits of information, and Val Cliffe produced some of the photographs. For the other illustrations, I am grateful to the Lancashire Library for granting me permission to use material from its archives and to the Editor of the *Nelson Leader*. Nicola Pike of Keele University Press has always been helpful in dealing with my questions and has orchestrated the production of the book every bit as expertly as she did a previous one. More recently, Nicola Carr of Edinburgh University Press has also been an invaluable link in the production process.

For much that might be of value in this study I must acknowledge the role of my editor, Stephen Constantine (no relation to Learie). Steve has been patient, encouraging and immensely perceptive. He has steered this book through difficult waters when he himself has had many more important things to worry about. His advice and support have been tremendous. He also knows where to place a comma.

My greatest debt, in this as in everything, is to the four people in the dedication.

Jeff Hill
Nottingham, February 1997

List of Tables

List of Abbreviations

AWA	Amalgamated Weavers' Association
CFT	*Cotton Factory Times*
CPGB	Communist Party of Great Britain
CSMA	Cotton Spinners' and Manufacturers' Association
ILP	Independent Labour Party
LRC	Labour Representation Committee
NC	*Nelson Chronicle*
NDMA	Nelson and District Manufacturers' Association
NG	*Nelson Gazette*
NL	*Nelson Leader*
NWA	Nelson Weavers' Association
PAC	Public Assistance Committee
SDF	Social-Democratic Federation
TUC	Trades Union Congress

1

Introduction:
Marsden to Nelson

> Nelson is undoubtedly a modern town. Fifty years ago it was entirely unknown, and no mention of it appears in any books dealing with the ancient history of the county.[1]

Three things are immediately striking about Nelson. First, it was essentially a creation of the later nineteenth century. It emerged from a group of small villages, none of which was precisely coterminous with the later settlement of Nelson. When the settlement did begin to take shape, its growth was rapid and it became a leading centre of cotton production in Lancashire and, as such, the world. Second, it has never been a large town. Its population has not risen beyond the 40,000 or so recorded in the 1921 census. These two features help to explain a third: Nelson's sense of itself as a distinctive place. Its rapid and late development, together with its size, created a feeling among Nelsonians that they lived in an exceptional, if not unique, community. Indeed, the idea of 'community' is particularly relevant in studying Nelson. Most places doubtless have a sense of their own importance, but in Nelson such a feeling seems to have been especially acute.

As one urban historian has noted, towns of the size and function of Nelson would have been important regional centres in most countries. In highly urbanised Britain, however, their size relegated them to 'comparatively inferior status'.[2] This certainly appears to have been the case with Nelson, reflected most clearly in the fact that only one book has so far recorded Nelson's development. This is Walter Bennett's *History of Marsden and Nelson*.[3] It is marvellously informative, but was written in the 1950s and therefore, stops at the point at which one of the town's most interesting developments – the decline of its staple industry – actually began. Moreover, Bennett devoted comparatively little space to what must be considered Nelson's most significant phase of growth, namely its industrial development from the 1870s to the 1930s. Instead, he concentrated most of his attention on the 'prehistory' of Nelson, chronicling in detail the history of the villages of Little and Great Marsden in the centuries before the Industrial Revolution. The present book, therefore, seeks to complement Bennett's work by

directing discussion to the years after the 1860s, which saw the mush-
rooming of the town of Nelson, the establishment of its cotton-based
economy, and its later economic and social reconstruction after the
Second World War.

Though Bennett's is the only book to date to have attempted a
general history of Nelson, the town has not been completely neglected
by historians. Indeed, four very important and different studies of the
town in its later period have been conducted. They deserve special
mention not only for their individual contribution to scholarship, but
also because they have each exercised an influence over the present
volume. To begin with, there is Jill Liddington's biography of Selina
Cooper, *The Life and Times of a Respectable Rebel*. This exceptional book
is more than just a study of the contribution made by a remarkable
woman to the local and national politics of the period between the
1890s and the 1940s. It is at the same a study of the place of women
in politics and society which stands as a leading example of how to
write the history of gender. It is also, to a great extent, a history of the
town of Nelson during this period, presenting a detailed account of
many facets of Nelson life, especially its politics. Alongside Liddington's
work is the study by Alan and Lesley Fowler of work and trade-unionism
in Nelson's principal industry – weaving: *The History of the Nelson
Weavers' Association*. The Fowlers cover the development of trade-
unionism in weaving in Nelson from its inception in the 1870s until
the union ceased to function as a separate entity in Nelson in the 1980s.
Their treatment of the industrial and political issues of the time,
especially of the confrontations of the late 1920s and 1930s, is – in an
overused historians' term which, in this case, is fully justified – definitive.
The two other works are doctoral theses and, therefore, were written
for a more specialist academic readership. Jane Mark-Lawson's thesis
deals with the subject of gender, politics and welfare during the period
1917 to 1934. It is a case-study of two towns of contrasting experiences
– Nelson and Luton. Mark-Lawson examines the interesting issue of
Nelson's distinctive provision of social services in the interwar years,
and her thesis offers important and original interpretations of Nelson
politics. Priscilla Ross, also in a doctoral thesis, has taken the theme of
workers, skill and technical change in Nelson since the late 19th century.
Among the many virtues of this work is the perspective that it gives of
the view from the loom, so to speak; that is to say, the working person's
angle on changes in the town's industry. In this context, the many oral
testimonies that Ross collected in the course of her work are richly
rewarding for the historian of Nelson.[4] For much of the time, the work
of preparing the present volume has been one of distilling and synthe-
sising the information and views presented in these four major studies,
together with the work of Bennett. The present book stands in all of
their shadows.

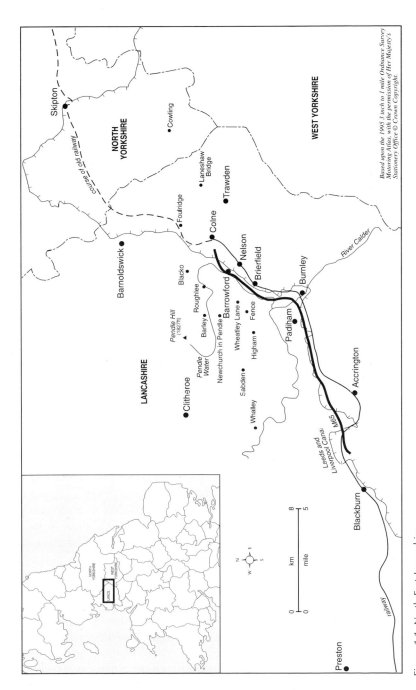

Based upon the 1995 3 inch to 1 mile Ordnance Survey
Motoring Atlas, with the permission of Her Majesty's
Stationery Office © Crown Copyright.

Figure 1.1 North-East Lancashire.

The relative neglect of Nelson by historians is typical of the gap
which British urban history in general has left in the area of the small
to medium-sized community. The omission is unfortunate for a number
of reasons. Perhaps the most important is the fact that many people
still live, and prefer to live, in communities of this size. The long-term
movement of people in Britain away from large cities, which began
after the Second World War and which has been described as a process
of 'decentralisation' of the population, has a number of causes but one
of them is undoubtedly the feeling that a better quality of life is to be
found in a smaller urban environment. Small communities are still,
therefore, a key part of the urban experience. Moreover, the fascination
with such places is not just a recent development. The small to medium-
sized provincial town – large enough to have its own dynamism, but
not so large that it loses a sense of community – has exercised a special
influence on people's imagination. In Britain, for example, it has often
been regarded as an ideal type of community. From the late nineteenth
century onwards, it has been the model for the balanced, harmonious
environments sought by town planners such as Ebenezer Howard,
Patrick Geddes and Lewis Mumford. Their ideas have been variously
expressed in the 'garden city' movement which produced Welwyn in
Hertfordshire and, from 1949 onwards, places such as Stevenage, Hemel
Hempstead, Cumbernauld and Skelmersdale, designed to accommodate
the 'overspill' from Britain's large cities. In some cases, of course, the
dream was not realised in practice; in spite of the architectural awards
lavished on them, the 'new towns' re-created many of the urban problems they were meant to solve. Nevertheless, the idea of the small town
as representing something qualitatively better, a higher form of civilis-
ation almost, lived on, not only in Britain. It had a powerful hold in
France, perhaps the country *par excellence* of the provincial town, and
was championed in the work of the Lyonnais architect Tony Garnier.
Similar sentiments were expressed in Germany by the economist and
planner A. F. Weber. The small-town dream reached its apotheosis in
America, celebrated in countless American films like William Wyler's
The Best Years of Our Lives, which, in 1946, significantly chose small-
town, middle America as the setting for the return of three ex-servicemen
to civilian 'normality'.[5]

If, in some cases, it was planning rather than size that was seen as
the defining feature of reconstructed urban life, there is no doubt that
notions of the ideal were being formed in contradistinction to the image
of the large, sprawling 'megalopolis'. Equally, however, it is clear that
the city – London especially, and the bigger provincial cities like
Manchester, Birmingham, Leeds and Liverpool – has captured the
historian's attention. Too often they are held to reflect national developments. But towns like Nelson can also help to illuminate important
trends in national history. In fact, in a book of this kind, it is the balance

between local and general that provides the crucial pitch of discussion. Indeed, the principal justification for a book on Nelson is the emphasis it brings (or restores, to be more precise) to the important urban form of the small town in the national community.

David F. Crew, writing about the growth of the German industrial town of Bochum during the late nineteenth and early twentieth centuries, indicated clearly the path that the historian must attempt to follow in striving for a balance between the local and the national: 'It is a question of asking how and in what ways and to what extent local areas participated in, contributed to, were affected by and reacted to the larger scale social, economic and political transformations that changed much of Europe during this period.'[6] Crew went further, pointing out that the local historian should develop a sensitivity to the unique without, at the same time, getting lost in it. In endeavouring to follow this advice, the present book adopts a twofold approach to its subject-matter.

On the one hand, it attempts to relate local developments to a broader pattern of national and international trends, often by reference to the debates that have been conducted among historians over the nature and significance of those trends. In this sense, Nelson is treated as a case-study against which general themes might be tested. On the other hand, however, the book attempts to plot the particular development of Nelson and to evaluate the changes that have taken place in the lives of its inhabitants. In this sense, it is concerned with the 'uniqueness' of the place, an overused notion perhaps, though, in the case of Nelson, at least partly justified. There are a number of features in Nelson's development that give the town a most distinctive appearance and, in themselves, are sufficient cause for a study of the place.

Nelson was one of those rare Victorian communities – Middlesbrough and Crewe were two others – which came into existence from virtually nothing. To the north-east of Blackburn and Accrington is an upland area of millstone grit, rising at its highest point (Pendle Hill) to over 550 metres. The area forms a quadrilateral, bounded by the medieval market centres of Burnley, Colne, Clitheroe and Whalley (see fig. 1.1). Between them is a landscape that has been aptly described as 'a peat-covered and rain-sodden wilderness'.[7] It was on the eastern side of this area that the town of Nelson developed in the later nineteenth century.

Historically, the area was a backwater. The early Celtic population of these parts seems to have been sparse, escaping the Roman influences which stopped at Ribchester, on the Ribble, some 20 miles to the south-west. It was colonised from Northumbria in the Anglo-Saxon period, as the profusion of place-names with the suffixes '-inga', '-inghaham' and '-ingatun' testifies. In medieval times it was an area given over largely to cattle farming in large vaccaries; the many 'booths' and

'folds' which remain in the place-names of the upland districts originated as summer pasturing. Not until the late Tudor period did its
economy begin to diversify in any significant way, with the development
of an interest in the production of woollen goods. This provided the

1.2 The pre-industrial past of the district around Nelson is illustrated by these seven-teenth-century houses in Barrowford. Bank Hall (opposite, top) dates from the late seventeenth century and, since the early years of the present century, has been a working men's club. The White Bear (opposite, bottom), dated 1607 but probably later, was, for many years, overshadowed by a cotton mill just behind it, which was the focus of 'more looms' demonstrations in 1931–32. Both were originally homes of relatively well-to-do families – the Sutcliffes and the Hargreaves respectively – who typically mixed pasture farming with an interest in textiles in this economic backwater. Park Hill (above), perhaps the most impressive example of the three, is an arche-typical Pennine manor house, with low-pitched roof, gables and heavily mullioned windows. It was built in the 1660s on land which had been owned by the Banastre (or Bannister) family since the fifteenth century. The Bannisters had been among the largest landowners in the district until their decline in the late seventeenth century. A later owner of Park Hill added an eighteenth-century extension on the profits of the worsted trade. Park Hill is now part of the Pendle Heritage Centre.

initial concern with textiles which, over the course of time, grew into the Victorian cotton town of Nelson.

Until the middle of the nineteenth century, only a few scattered households were to be encountered in that part of north-east Lancashire which lay between the two medieval settlements of Burnley and Colne within the ecclesiastical parish of Whalley. The principal settlements were Little and Great Marsden, Barrowford, Trawden and Foulridge, surrounded by a string of smaller villages which, in many cases, had been cattle pastures in former times (see fig. 1.1). (Map 1) Until the improvement of communications in the later eighteenth century, with the construction of roads and canals to facilitate the export of Bradford

woollens,[8] this remote corner of Lancashire had known an impover-
ished, semi-subsistence economic life. It shared in few of the economic
changes that brought material improvements to other parts of England.
It was a district of meagre arable and sheep farming, dominated by a
few small gentry families such as the Bannisters of Park Hall, Barrowford, probably the richest family in the area until the late seventeenth
century; the Waltons of Marsden Hall, and their relations, the Sagars
of Catlow; the Hartleys of Bradley End; and the Ridehalghs of Scholefield. Their local reputation had become established following the
acquisition of copyhold status in the sixteenth century. They still owned
land by the end of the eighteenth, but now supplemented their income
from the trade in textiles.[9] Since the late sixteenth century, as already
noted, the local economy had become reliant upon the supplementing
of marginal farming by the domestic production of woollen textiles. By
the eighteenth century this was beginning to replace agriculture as the
major source of livelihood. Fustians – a mixture of wool and cotton –
became the staple output of the district, and most of them were
produced, even into the early nineteenth century, on handlooms in
domestic premises. In addition, spinning continued to provide a source
of income, and some coal was mined at Marsden. By the first half of
the nineteenth century the district was established as a series of small
agricultural-cum-industrial villages whose population was rising until,
in the 1840s, the development of cotton production in the factory
system began to drain people away from some of the smaller places
(see Table 1.1). It was in this inhospitable country, dominated by Pendle
Hill and its associations with witchcraft, that the Victorian new town
of Nelson emerged in the last thirty years of the nineteenth century,
around the nucleus of villages centred on the two Marsdens.

Table 1.1. Population of the Marsden District, 1801–1851

	1801	1811	1821	1831	1841	1851
Little Marsden			2051	2742	3171	3997
Great Marsden			1893	1971	1987	2071
Barrowford	1224	1721	2168	2633	2630	2875
Trawden	1443	1941	2507	2853	2900	2601
Foulridge	833	1032	1307	1418	1458	1233
Wheatley Carr	42	65	69	58	53	40
Old Laund Booth	257	316	390	476	481	447
Roughlee Booth	684	795	958	949	782	719
Goldshaw Booth	516	626	819	763	748	620
Barley with Wheatley Booth	528	566	765	707	686	542

Source: *Census of Great Britain, 1851* (London, 1852).

To the acute Victorian observer, the emergence of Nelson would not have been surprising. A number of advantages explain the establishment there, from the 1870s onwards, of a cotton industry which rapidly came to specialise in weaving. Firstly, during the previous generation, the nearby towns of Burnley and Colne had already undergone that process of transition from woollen cloth production, through the handloom manufacture of cotton cloths, to a system of factory production of cotton by power-looms.[10] Their economic success, especially that of Burnley, provided an impetus for further regional development, and the Marsden district seemed a natural place for overspill. A second advantage accrued from the availability of cheap land for both industrial premises and the houses for those who worked in them. Local quarries provided the building materials for the distinctive millstone grit/sandstone terraces that began to appear in the 1870s. The characteristic feature of the district's industrial architecture – the expansive, single-storey weaving shed (rather than the multi-storey structures found in the spinning districts of south Lancashire) – is also explained by the same factors, relative cheapness of land and local stone. A third contributory factor in the district's economic development arose from its communications. It stood at the intersection of a north–south road connecting Burnley to Skipton, through Colne, and the road striking east to Halifax (see fig. 1.1). In addition, water-borne traffic was made possible by the Leeds–Liverpool canal, constructed from the late eighteenth century and finally completed in 1816.[11] Furthermore, by 1849 the East Lancashire Railway had extended its line from Burnley through Colne in order to link up with the Midland Railway's Bradford to Skipton branch. The company opened a station near a public house – the Nelson Inn – on the Burnley to Colne road. The commercial motive for the station was the business expected from the mills in Barrowford, but it was the arrival of the railway which also brought about the renaming of the settlement. According to the Victorian writer W. A. Abram, the railway company was undecided on a name for the station, built on an area formerly known as 'Hibson's Farm'. It eventually adopted 'Nelson' because the only significant landmark in the immediate vicinity was the Nelson Inn, a coaching stop dating from the early nineteenth century commemorating the famous naval hero. 'Nelson' became the name applied increasingly to the district in the following years, as the focus of economic activity shifted away from Little and Great Marsden to the area around the railway. It was, however, an unofficial designation, for no publicly recognised area known as 'Nelson' existed as yet. This was partly rectified in 1864, when Nelson received its first official acknowledgement as an urban entity. This came with the formation of a Local Board – 'for the district of Nelson', as recorded in the *London Gazette* – to administer the affairs of an area including parts of the townships of Great and Little Marsden, Barrowford and

Wheatley Carr. This was, in essence, the area of 'Nelson' as it had come
to be known by the early 1860s. But it was not until 1890 that a charter
of incorporation was obtained, giving Nelson municipal borough status
with six wards which together defined the area of the borough. In 1894
the old township of Marsden was dismantled and its former parts added
to the borough of Colne and to the new townships of Brierfield and
Nelson, the latter accounting in 1901 for over 32,000 of the population
of the former Marsden. By this gradual process of identification, Nelson
became probably the only English town of any size to be named after
a pub.

Two further factors explain why the opportunities for development
offered by these conditions were seized. The first was the presence of
a broadly based class of small capitalists. Insofar as the district had
inherited a resident bourgeoisie, it existed in the form of the established
manufacturers of Burnley and Colne, together with the local gentry of
the Marsden area. Some of the latter group, like the Quaker family of
Lomeshaye, the Ecroyds, had already moved into textile manufacturing
by the later eighteenth century, gaining a reputation for the production
of high-quality woollens. Others, such as members of the Sagar and
Walton families, saw opportunities for investment in factory textile
production from the middle of the nineteenth century, often in partnership with 'new' men from outside the area whose profits from property
building or the coal trade were also channelled into textiles. A distin-
guishing feature of the enterprise of these groups was a division of
functions known as the 'room and power' system. It brought together
two types of owners: on the one hand, there were the builders and
owners of mill premises; on the other hand, renting space in the mills,
there were the owners of looms who were also the employers of the
labour necessary to operate them. Start-up costs for the latter were
modest, therefore, since they did not have to find the additional capital
for constructing mill buildings. This provided a relatively open entry
to the business of cotton production and encouraged a variety of entrepreneurs, some of them from quite humble origins. The resultant
wide-ranging diffusion of the means of production prevented the dominance of the cotton trade by a closed group of wealthy owners, such
as occurred in other Lancashire towns, and had far-reaching effects on
the social and political, as well as the economic, development of Nelson.

The second factor highlights the necessary stimulus to this business
initiative: the availability of cheap labour. Little in the way of alternative
employment was available in the area. Agriculture simply did not have
the natural endowments to expand beyond its narrow limits of essentially pasture farming. Indeed, the traditional resort to textiles as an
additional source of income meant that spinning and weaving skills had
been developed locally for generations, and were now available to
service the new factories. The decline of the handloom in the face of

both competition from the more productive power-loom and the economies of scale to be derived from the factory method of production was inevitable after the 1840s, though probably at a less rapid rate than has sometimes been supposed.[12] However, local weavers in the villages of the Lancashire–Yorkshire border, who had earlier resisted the lure of Burnley and Colne, had little option by the 1860s but to take the road to Nelson.

There was indeed a ready supply of this labour. By the 1880s, Nelson was a town of immigrants. Most of them had arrived from settlements nearby. Census returns from the 1870s and 1880s constantly note the loss of population from villages on the Lancashire–Yorkshire border 'in consequence of the removal of families to other parts to seek employment', as the census of 1851 noted. In the 1870s, the area near the Old Salem Chapel in Nelson was known as 'New Trawden' because most of the people living there had migrated from the village of 'old' Trawden during the previous 20 years. In fact, research by M. E. W. Brooker suggests that, in the 1860s, some 70 per cent of migrants to Nelson arrived from destinations no more than five miles distant.[13] Personal histories help to underline this process. The Snowden family of Cowling, some seven miles away, was an illustrious case in point. In his autobiography, written in the 1930s, the former Labour Cabinet minister Philip Snowden described how his family left the Yorkshire upland village of Cowling in the 1880s, when the mill at which his father worked went bankrupt, and removed to the new town. 'At that time', Snowden commented, 'the town of Nelson ... was attracting people from the West Riding, where the woollen trade was very depressed.'[14] Where the Snowdens were exceptional was in the fact that they did not stay long in Nelson. Philip moved on after a few years to a post in the Civil Service. His father died and his mother moved back to Cowling. For most immigrants at this time, Nelson remained their home. At the opposite extreme geographically from people like the Snowdens was a significant migration of miners and their families from Cornwall. As Cornwall's tin and copper mines closed down in the 1860s, faced with foreign competition, a mass exodus occurred, with many making the journey north. Burnley, an expanding cotton town with a large mining sector, attracted many families, some of whom found their way to nearby towns and villages such as Barnoldswick, Brierfield, and Nelson. One such family was that of a Cornish railway navvy whose various members made their way, in separate small groups, to north-east Lancashire during the course of the late 1860s and 1870s. One daughter, Selina Coombe, born in the same year as Philip Snowden, went straight into the mill on arriving in Barnoldswick in 1876 and then moved to Brierfield in 1883 to work at Tunstill's mill. She moved to Nelson in 1896, after marrying Robert Cooper, a postman who had left Swaledale in North Yorkshire and followed an elder brother into the town.[15] Selina Cooper did not, like Philip Snowden, achieve high office, but she went on to exercise a considerable influence on Nelson's politics for many years.

In this way, Nelson acquired its expanded population. By 1861 the population of Great and Little Marsden had risen to 7,342 and, by 1871, to 10,284 as a result of increasing migration into the new districts of Nelson and Brierfield. This continued, with a sharp increase between 1881 and 1891 from 16,725 to 31,339. In 1894 the registration districts were altered, so that, by the time of the 1901 census, Nelson had become a separate sub-district (including parts of Barrowford, Wheatley Carr and Brierfield) with a population of 32,717. By 1911 the population had increased still further to 39,479. Whilst it is clear that inward migration accounted for a major part of this increase, the precise orgins of the migrants are difficult to determine, since at this time the census recorded no data on the birthplaces of the inhabitants of districts with a population of less than 50,000. Some general indications can be gleaned, however, from the figures recorded for the Urban Sanitary District of Burnley, which included Nelson. Table 1.2 shows percentages for both Burnley and Nelson together. These data confirm the picture of the Marsden–Nelson district as an economic magnet, attracting labour especially from a host of nearby communities. Some of these people doubtless came from existing manufacturing centres like Burnley and Colne; others from semi–industrial villages. In all cases, it was the

Table 1.2. Birthplaces of Inhabitants in the Burnley Urban Sanitary District, 1891 (%)

Eastern counties	0.4
London	0.3
N Midland counties	0.8
Northern counties	1.5
NW counties	78.5
SE counties	0.3
S Midland counties	0.4
SW counties	2.5[a]
Wales (inc. Monmouth)	0.3
W Midland counties	1.2
Yorkshire	8.5
Others	5.3

Note: Populations for Nelson and Burnley were 22,700 and 58,751 respectively.
[a] This included 1.9% from Cornwall.
Source: *Census of England and Wales 1891* (London, 1892).

prospect of better wages in the burgeoning weaving trade of Nelson that was the attraction. Their presence vindicated the initiative of small manufacturers in setting up mills in this district.

The town to which these migrants came was blessed with a striking natural landscape which shaped its built environment. Nelson lies to the east and south of a valley formed by Pendle Water. The land rises sharply to the south-east, from around 100 metres above sea level in the valley bottom to some 185 metres within a mile (see figs 1.3 and 1.4).

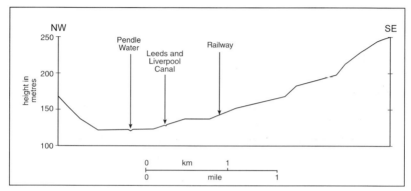

Figure 1.3 Cross-section through Nelson.

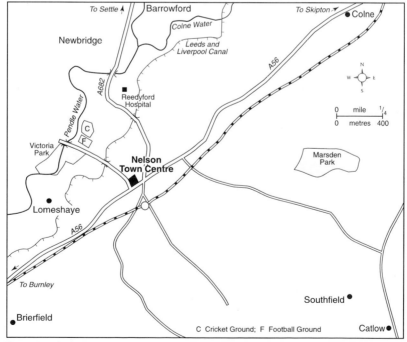

Figure 1.4 Nelson, c.1945.

Urban growth was most noticeable to the south and east of the valley and its road and railway line, in an arc encompassing the old districts of Little Marsden, Walverden and Hendon. There was no significant expansion beyond Pendle Water, which still remains an area of open moorland with a clear view to Pendle Hill.

By the eve of the First World War, the physical shape of Nelson was more or less complete. It changed remarkably little over the years before the Second World War (see fig. 1.5). So too did the urban appearance of the town, until reconfigured by the redevelopment of the central area and the motorway building of the 1970s and 1980s. Nelson was a compact town. The longest extent of the built-up area was about 2½ miles, from the edge of Brierfield to the beginnings of Colne, at Primet Bridge, along the Manchester and Leeds roads. From the southern edge of the industrial village of Barrowford in the north-west, still a distinctly separate community even today, to the most south-easterly point of Nelson, at Scholefield, was a distance of approximately two miles. This confined development made for an urban area with the potential for a sense of community. Townspeople were, by and large, in close proximity to each other. It was the kind of place where it might be – and, indeed, was – said that 'everybody knew everybody else's business'. Though housing and industrial development took Nelson to the very boundaries of the neighbouring settlements of Barrowford, Colne and Brierfield, there was nonetheless a sufficiently clear space between these other communities and Nelson for the traveller to be aware of separate townships.

Within Nelson, a number of topographical features helped to instil a sense of community among its inhabitants. One pervasive characteristic of the town, for example, was the proximity of open countryside. From virtually everywhere, a view of something beyond Nelson was available; from some of the highest points in the borough, that view could be spectacular – as from the 1920s housing estate in Ringstone Crescent across the valley to Pendle Hill. The town itself might have possessed few aesthetic qualities of a built nature, but its natural situation was enviable. The architectural historian Nikolaus Pevsner summed it up: 'Nelson has no past and no architectural shape ... The centre of Nelson is entirely inarticulate ... However, the moors are near, and that makes up for much.' [16]

By 1914 the town's appearance was, to be sure, utilitarian. But this also created a kind of uniformity of experience. Five roads fanned out from the central crossroads by the Nelson Inn, which was the town's initial *raison d'être*; their names described their purposes – Leeds, Railway, Manchester, Market and (somewhat ambitiously) Scotland. A cluster of unprepossessing civic buildings lay just to the west of the centre, forming a municipal precinct, though without anything that could be described as a public open space. Bordering this area was the

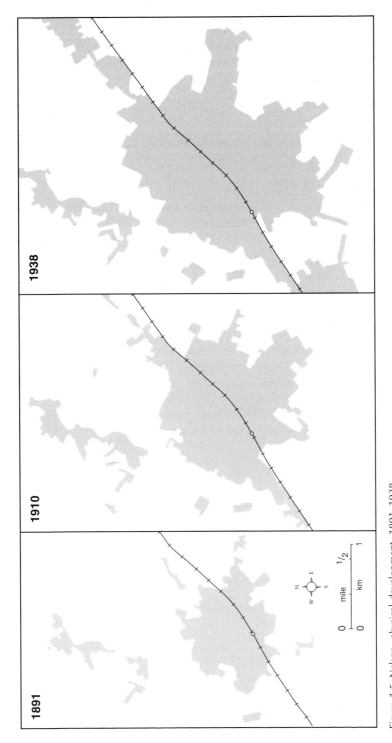

1891   **1910**   **1938**

Figure 1.5 Nelson: physical development, 1891–1938.

1.6 Carr Road, looking north-west towards Pendle Hill, *c*.1914 (top). Are these people leaving a cricket match, or a fair, or just promenading? At the bottom of the hill is Victoria Park, the recreation ground, and the cricket and football fields at Seedhill. The area thus formed one of the town's main recreational districts. (*Lancashire Library, Nelson Local Studies Collection*).

   Some eighty years later (bottom), the old football ground has gone, the Imperial Ballroom has come and gone, and the M65 motorway has appeared. Pendle Hill remains in the distance and some beautiful country is still within a short walking distance.

1.7 Nelson centre in the early years of the present century. Five roads met at this point, which was described (rather grandiloquently) in 1910 as 'the hub of a great industrial wheel; (*Nelson Leader*, 11 March 1910). It had provided the geographical rationale for Nelson's emergence as a town in the second half of the nineteenth century. The railway station is a short distance away and the (new) Lord Nelson Hotel (formerly the Nelson Inn) is to the photographer's right. With the increase in road traffic and the advent of the electric tramcar service to Colne and Barrowford, it was not advisable to stand for too long in the middle of the road. Nelson never possessed a central open space in which pedestrians could congregate until this very area was sealed off to traffic some 70 years after this photograph was taken. (*Lancashire Library, Nelson Local Studies Collection*)

shopping district, confined principally to Market Street, Scotland Road and Manchester Road. Industrial premises and their attendant workers' housing encroached upon the centre, creating a pattern for the whole of the town. In other words, everywhere looked much the same. With the exception of an area on the edge of the town, in the lower ground by Pendle Water, where recreation-ground, football and cricket fields, and a public park had been created to form an area for outdoor pastimes, there were no discernibly separate areas within the town. For example, there was no distinct middle-class suburb of superior housing with gardens, such as might be found in many other towns, even those of a similar size to Nelson. Small pockets of 'better-class' housing were scattered throughout the town. Even the grander homes of the few élite families were to be found cheek by jowl with factories and terraced, garden-less houses. The home of William Tunstill, Reedyford Hall, was within a mile of the centre of Nelson, on the boundaries of Nelson and Barrowford; it gained seclusion from being in a relatively large, wooded site rather than being at a distance from the town itself. Not

1.8 An aerial view of Nelson centre, taken in 1953. The basic configuration of the town centre has scarcely changed at all since the early years of the century. The cluster of municipal buildings is located in the lower centre of the picture; particularly evident is the proximity to the central area of mill buildings, with their characteristic 'saw-tooth' roofing designs. (*Lancashire Library, Nelson Local Studies Collection*)

until the inter-war period did Amos Nelson, proprietor of the town's largest manufacturing concern by this time, forsake the town altogether, leaving his house in Barkerhouse Road and taking up residence in the Yorkshire Dales, from where he motored into Nelson each day to conduct his business.

There was, therefore, a uniformity of appearance to the built environment – with mill buildings and terraced houses the predominant feature – which might have helped to instil a common, if not egalitarian, feeling among the townspeople of Nelson. Aerial photographs were later to bring out this appearance quite starkly, showing the rigidly laid-out rows of houses and the local mills which their occupants served. However, as in many other cotton towns, the homogeneity of the urban architecture could belie the existence of separate communities within the whole. Whilst the compactness of the town no doubt helped to foster a sense of civic community, the topography also a encouraged neighbourhood mentalities. Steep gradients and the proximity of work, corner shops and schools militated against excessive cross-town journeys. Although the market, 'big' shops, places of entertainment and many chapels were all located in the centre – making travel into 'Nelson' a necessity from time to time – there was still enough to sustain a daily life in the various localities, whose identities were kept alive by the culture of mill, chapel, Sunday school, pub and the meeting place provided by the ubiquitous chip shop, always open at both midday and 'teatime'. Nelson, therefore, possessed the physical configurations that allowed both an idea of 'town' and of loyalties within the town to flourish. This was to be a marked feature of the community's development.

2

The Mill Economy:
Entrepreneurs and Workers,
1870–1914

By sheer pluck and energy its people have raised the town within a
few years from a comparatively insignificant position to one of conspicuous importance.[1]

The most striking feature of Nelson's growth in the late nineteenth
century was unquestionably its rapidity. In the early 1870s the scattered
households and mills of the district accounted for a population of some
10,000. By 1900 the borough of Nelson was an established centre of
cotton production, with a population in excess of 30,000. Over 20 mills
contained somewhere in the region of 26,000 looms, with 70 per cent
of the workforce engaged in various processes of cotton textile production, almost exclusively concerned with the manufacturing of cotton
cloths.

The development of Nelson from the 1870s illustrates an often
overlooked aspect of the British economy at this time. Nelson represented a growth point in a national economy which was otherwise
beginning to slow down after a period of boom in the earlier years of
the century. Having been the first country to industrialise from the
end of the eighteenth century, establishing itself by the 1850s and 1860s
as the principal source of manufacturing output in the world – 'the
workshop of the world' – Britain began to encounter some of the disadvantages of having been first in the field. Overseas competitors – the
USA and the bigger continental European countries in particular –
were challenging Britain's position, mainly by protecting their nascent
industries behind tariff walls. The effect of this was the circumscription
of British exports in world markets by the 1890s. Within Britain,
repercussions were felt in the form of reduced profit margins in business
which in turn prompted a general attempt by employers to reduce
labour costs. The effects of this were seen in industrial relations, which
generally worsened during the last decade of the century, with a number
of legal cases challenging various aspects of trade-union activitity. Some
voices were also raised in favour of the protection of British industry.

The idea was eventually adopted by the Conservative Party in 1903, when, following pressure from Joseph Chamberlain, it abandoned its traditional adherence to the principle of free trade. Curiously, one of the earliest champions of protectionism was the Nelson manufacturer W. F. Ecroyd. He had established steam-powered mills at Lomeshaye in the mid-nineteenth century and employed former handloom weavers to manufacture 'Bradford' (i.e. woollen) cloths.

However, it was to be cotton, rather than woollen, goods which became Nelson's staple trade, and cotton cloth manufacture escaped much of the turmoil that affected other branches of British industry in the late nineteenth century – at least, the more specialised and quality-based weaving firms did, and it was this form of manufacture that became established in Nelson. The town in effect took over the market for sateens and greys, which had previously been located in south Lancashire, in Ashton-under-Lyne, but lost there following a serious strike in the 1870s.[2] By 1886, one fifth of all Nelson looms were weaving sateens and fancies.[3] At a time when Lancashire cotton generally was losing its grip on the North American and European markets and coming to rely increasingly on the Indian and Chinese trade, Nelson was developing specialisms which enabled its cloths to be sold in a more competitive and lucrative arena. By the beginning of the twentieth century, most mills in Nelson were weaving a range of specialist cloths which included flannelettes, poplins, moreens, twills, coloured stripes, ginghams, regattas and handkerchiefs as well as the specialisms of Venetians, Florentines and cotton Italians. Ecroyds still produced high-quality woollen goods for the London and US markets. As a result of this, Nelson's manufacturers were able to sell their goods in a diversified international and domestic market. They were therefore spared some of the more violent fluctuations in demand which characterised the coarse trade of towns like Blackburn, whose business was done chiefly in cheap goods for the Far East market. Between the 1880s and the First World War, therefore, Nelson enjoyed relative stability and prosperity, the most trouble-free period of its industrial history.

Although Nelson's textile industry had initially been a mixed one, the process by which spinning was replaced by weaving was a rapid one. The reasons are clear. Looms were cheaper to obtain and quicker to install than self-actor spinning mules. They required less technical knowledge to operate, and labour was in ready supply. Trade-unionism among weavers was less well-established than in spinning, where the Spinners' Amalgamation had acquired a reputation by the 1880s for enforcing wage lists and controlling entry into the trade in a determined manner. It is not surprising, therefore, that a newly developing district like Nelson should have seen greater advantages in weaving. As Farnie has pointed out, no spinning concerns were set up in the town after 1887 and, by the mid-1890s, Nelson was importing from other parts of Lancashire virtually all (98 per cent) of the yarn its weaving sheds were consuming.[4]

Opportunities had been seized in a classic Victorian individualist fashion. Nelson's growth was achieved through a process of *laissez-faire*, private and largely speculative initiatives of an essentially small-scale nature. It was testimony to what, a hundred years later, was being reinvented in some political quarters as 'Victorian values'. The basis of capital accumulation was (for this period) comparatively small. Entrepreneurs took advantage of cheap building land and the provisions of the limited liability legislation of the 1862 Companies Act, which enabled groups of businessmen to raise capital on the share principle. The weaving trade was characterised, as we saw in Chapter 1, by that distinctive separation of entrepreneurial functions embodied in the 'room and power' system. As Alan and Lesley Fowler have pointed out, this system (sometimes known as 'space and turning') was employed 'on a scale not seen in any other Lancashire town of its size'.[5] In a survey of the rise of the cotton trade in the district, published in the *Colne and Nelson Times* in 1911, the Landless brothers were credited with the introduction of 'room and power' in the mid-1860s. As owners of a foundry and an engineering business, set up on land purchased from the Towneley family, they diverted some of their capital into the building of mill premises in which space could be let to owners of looms. This speculative beginning was followed by local builders Whitehead and Holland, who set up Victoria Mill on similar lines shortly afterwards.[6] Reginald Elliott, another local builder, similarly constructed a mill in Netherfield Road. The Tunstill brothers, William and Robert, whose father had originally come to Nelson from nearby Wheatley Lane, formed a limited company to build Bradley Mill. Such ventures resulted in the registering of ten mill companies in Nelson between 1875 and 1896.[7] The initiators were usually businessmen who, like the Landless brothers, had either made their money outside cotton or who had made profits by producing cloth in the room and power system and then decided to move into mill ownership. Examples of the latter type were John Whittaker, who had rented space at Albert Mills before building Seed Hill Mills and taking 800 of its 1,200 looms there himself, letting the remaining space to others; and James Nelson, whose firm ('Jimmy Nelson's' of Valley Mills) was to become the largest weaving undertaking in the town by the early years of the twentieth century. Jimmy Nelson represents, albeit in an exaggerated form, that same transformation from modest beginnings to mill owner that was experienced by so many other Nelson manufacturers at this time. His story is worth considering.

James Nelson had worked as the manager of a mill in the village of Winewall, near Colne, until the age of 50, when, in 1881, his employers decided to close down. Having saved the considerable sum of £1,000

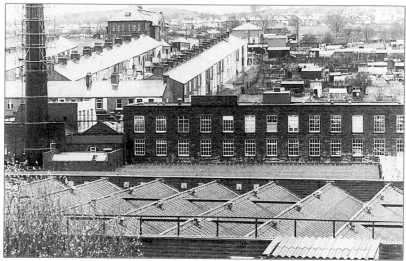

2.1 Valley Mills, home of 'Jimmy Nelson's'. The founder personified the Victorian self-help ideal, having risen from a modest position as a mill manager to become the owner of the largest cotton-weaving concern in Nelson by the time of his death in 1912. It was after this that the firm blossomed, however, under the leaderhip of Nelson's son, Amos, who was knighted in 1922. During the First World War Nelson's quality ribbed poplins were in great demand from the Forces; wartime profits enabled the firm to develop new marketing and production techniques in the 1920s which transformed it into a company operating on a national basis. It was Nelson's who took the step out of cotton weaving into rayon production, a move which helped to circumvent the problem of foreign competition and to mitigate the effects of the inter-war economic depression in Nelson. (*Lancashire Library, Nelson Local Studies Collection*)

during the course of some 40 years of working life, Nelson decided to put this money into a business of his own. He rented space for 160 looms at Brook Street Mills in Nelson, a company formed through a partnership between Joseph Sunderland and his friend Thomas Hargreaves, a corn dealer from Burnley. Because of commitments to his former employers which prevented James Nelson from working full-time at his new firm, he entrusted the supervision of his business to his son Amos, whom he had schooled in the weaving trade. Though accounts of his subsequent progress vary in detail, it seems clear that, by the end of the 1880s, the Nelsons had somewhere in the region of 1,000 looms running in the town, mostly at Walverden Shed, one of the four original cotton factories in the district dating back to the pre-room and power days of the 1850s.[8] In 1895 James Nelson was financially strong enough to dispense with the room and power arrangement and build his own mill – No. 1 Mill of Valley Mills – and, by the end of the century, to have completed a second shed. At first Valley Mills themselves offered space on the room and power principle to other producers, but it was not long before they housed exclusively

Nelsons' looms. Though they wove both American and Egyptian yarns for the Chinese market, Nelsons made their name manufacturing fine-quality goods, initially a 54-inch Italian cloth for menswear linings, which was sold both abroad and at home. Cotton Venetians with the trade names 'Marquise', 'Marquise de Luxe' and 'Marquise Sunbrite' did especially well in America. Specialisation in these fine lines was taken further during the early years of the new century with the production of poplins for dresses and shirts, also marketed both at home and abroad. By 1910 the firm was manufacturing between 300,000 and 400,000 yards of all types of cloth each week and beginning to move into a process of 'backward integration'. To secure the supply of yarn in the face of big demand for their cloths, Nelsons started to acquire interests in the spinning trade. Mills were purchased in both of the main spinning centres – Bolton and Rochdale – and this process continued after the First World War, by which time James Nelson's company was no longer simply what it had started out as – a weaving firm based in the town of Nelson. James Nelson, who died in 1912, at the point at which his firm was breaking out of its local confines, had been immensely successful. He showed what could be achieved from a small beginning by a determined and skilful Victorian entrepreneur.[9]

By the eve of the First World War, there were 31 separate mills in Nelson, containing some 111 manufacturing concerns. In only a few cases – that of the Ecroyds' company at Lomeshaye was one, alongside Nelsons – was the ownership of the mill and the manufacture of the cloth in the same hands.[10] The room and power system had its advantages, but it also had drawbacks. It allowed producers to set up relatively easily, with a minimum of capital, often borrowed, for looms, yarn and wages. It was usually possible to obtain an initial consignment of yarn on credit from the suppliers, and an advance could often be obtained from the Manchester cloth merchants against a favourable price for the first output of cloth. This covered the wages bill for first two or three weeks. Thereafter, the rent for room and power varied according to the state of trade, but was usually 35s.–42s. (£1.75–£2.10) a week per loom. However, whilst the system offered the prospect of speedy access to cotton production, 'room and power' as a basis for a local economy posed many obstacles to sustained industrial development. Short-term success, it later emerged, was bought at the expense of longer-term viability. Many of the small manufacturers who entered the trade were forced to operate at the very margins of profitability, constantly short of capital and dependent upon credit during times of poor trade or industrial conflict. As economic 'actors', they were in a weak position in relation to a series of other agents in the market-place; first, their suppliers, the yarn merchants, principally supplying Egyptian yarn spun in Bolton, who often sold at high prices for immediate cash payment; second, their buyers, the cloth agents, who controlled the price of the finished product; and third, but not least in importance, their labour, who, following the growth of strong trade-unionism in the district, sought to enforce stringent deals over both wages and working conditions in the mills.

Not surprisingly, in view of these factors, weaving was a trade characterised by a high turnover of producers. For every success story, such as that of James Nelson, there were many failures. It must be doubted whether the oft-repeated myth of the small man making good in weaving had much substance to it. Nevertheless, the system as a whole worked – and on a smaller-scale basis than in other weaving towns. The 111 manufacturers listed in Barrett's *Directory* of the Nelson district just before the First World War varied in size from the bigger firms like James Nelson, Walter Reed, Ridehalgh, Ecroyd and John Wilkinson, all with over 1,000 looms, to very small enterprises – John W. Pickles, for example, weaving sateens at Bradley Shed with just 22 looms. Even the large firms were not big by contemporary industrial standards. The 1,200 looms and 24,000 doubling spindles at Nelson's Valley Mills, though it was to grow into a bigger company in later years, represented a tiny operation by comparison with some of the corporate giants of the British economy, such as Vickers' engineering firm. Even when gauged by the scale of operations in other weaving towns, Nelson's average of 437 looms per firm was much lower than Burnley (715) or Blackburn (822). In 1911, only 4 per cent of the town's firms possessed over 1,000 looms.[11]

By this time, just before the War, with almost all the cotton production in Nelson based on weaving, the town had risen to be the third largest producer of cotton cloths after Burnley and Blackburn. The last concern to be devoted solely to spinning had closed in 1887.[12] The town stood as a clear example of the localised horizontal integration that had been taking place in the Lancashire cotton industry over the previous twenty years and which, in Nelson, had worked to eliminate almost all diversity from the local economy.

Cotton weaving also had its own distinctive characteristics. Architecture and technology were two of its more obvious hallmarks. As Joseph and Frank Nasmith, the early historians of cotton mill building, showed, the relative cheapness of land in north-east Lancashire encouraged the building of low, sprawling weaving sheds, with their characteristic 'saw tooth' design of north-facing windows set into the roofs.[13] Such design was consistent with the financial context in which the trade operated. Among the advantages of this type of construction was the steady north light that it offered at the level of each loom, allied to the avoidance of direct sunlight, which would have been detrimental to the weaving of coloured cloths. It also kept building costs to a minimum by eliminating the need for windows in the walls. The specific piece of machinery housed in these sheds was

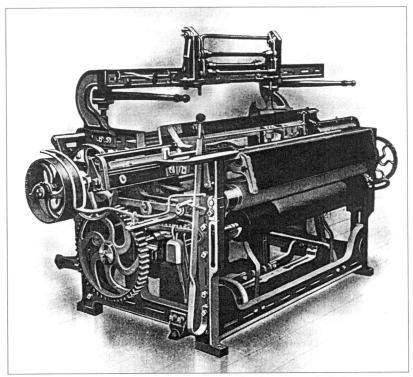

2.2 The steam-powered Lancashire loom – the technology upon which the success of Nelson's mills depended. Power-looms were known from the end of the eighteenth century, but were not adopted generally until towards the middle of the nineteenth century. Nelson, as a 'new' town, had this technology from the outset, though by the 1890s it had been superseded technically by the more advanced automatic looms developed in America. Whereas 1 weaver usually tended 4 of the Lancashire looms, up to 24 of the newer automatic machines could be supervised by a single weaver. Few Lancashire manufacturers attempted to replace the power-loom, however, especially in Nelson, where it was felt to be more suitable for weaving the finer cloths in which the town specialised. Modified in the inter-war period to enable it to run more efficiently and, therefore, to require fewer weavers, the Lancashire loom survived into the post-1945 era, until scrapped *en masse* following the Cotton Industry Act of 1959.

the Lancashire loom. This was the steam-powered technology that had been responsible for ousting the handloom during the third quarter of the nineteenth century. By the beginning of the twentieth century – and certainly by the 1920s – it was backward in its technological sophistication by comparison with the equipment used in newer cotton industries overseas. The Lancashire loom and the self-actor mule (the mainstay of yarn production), produced in their thousands by Lancashire mill engineering firms like Platt Brothers of Oldham, had come to seem crude when judged against the American-invented Northrop automatic loom and the ring-spinning processes being adopted

elsewhere. Historians have argued over the extent to which this technological backwardness was responsible for Lancashire cotton's eventual
decline. Certainly, the Northrop loom – introduced in the USA in the
1890s, but not in evidence in any numbers in Lancashire until the 1920s
– had two distinct advantages over the old power-loom. In the first
place, it both repaired snapped warp and replaced yarn in the shuttle
without the need for the weaver to stop the loom. It therefore reduced
the number of hitches in the weaving process. Secondly, and consequently, use of the Northrop loom permitted the supervision of a
greater number of looms by the same number of weavers, allowing a
significant saving to be made on labour costs.[14] As may be imagined,
the issue of installing the Northrop loom at the expense of the Lancashire loom became a crucial one in the interwar period. Before 1914,
in relatively prosperous conditions, most manufacturers (and especially
small ones lacking capital) felt inclined to stay with the technology they
were used to; after all, it had seen towns like Nelson rise to a leading
place in the world's cotton trade. If, as was often remarked, 'Britain's
bread hung by Lancashire's thread', it seemed equally true that
Nelson's bread was produced on the Lancashire loom.

By the time of the First World War, some 75 per cent of the
workforce in Nelson and its neighbouring villages of Brierfield and
Barrowford were dependent upon weaving for their livelihood. No
other occupation even remotely rivalled this trade in terms of the
amount of employment it offered. The only other significant numbers
of workers were to be found in metalworking (2 per cent of the labour
force in Nelson), transport and communications (2.6 per cent), various
branches of commerce (4.5 per cent) and domestic service (1.8 per
cent).[15] In having this preponderance of workers in one trade, Nelson
was exceptional, though not unique, among Lancashire towns. Places
like Walton-le-Dale (textiles) and Haydock (coal mining) were equally
dependent upon a single trade.

Nelson's difference lay in the fact that, unlike most other towns in
which weaving was carried out, it was not regarded here as an occupation
exclusively for *women*.[16] In Nelson, weaving employed men and women
in almost equal proportions. In fact, Chapman's classic study of the
cotton industry, conducted in the early years of the twentieth century,
showed Nelson to be one of only three Lancashire cotton towns (the
others were Colne and Royton) where there were fewer females than
males in the textile labour force.[17] The census of 1921, taken at what
was the peak of employment in the cotton industry locally, recorded
just under 19,500 people employed in the various branches of cotton
production in Nelson itself; 17,299 (88.9 per cent) were classified as
working in weaving, of whom 9,975 (57.6 per cent) were female and
7,324 (42.3 per cent) male. There were, to be sure, significant gender
differences in the other branches of cotton. Aside from winding, where

80 per cent of the workforce was female, the trades of doubling, sizing, twisting and drawing, and cloth-looking were almost exclusively male.[18] However, since the combined workforce in all these other trades accounted for only 11 per cent of the total labour force in cotton production, the male bias in these trades was heavily counterbalanced by the situation among the weavers, which did present a general case of equal opportunities. This was a feature of the local labour market that had far-reaching consequences upon the social and political development of the town.

Above all, it meant that the status of women in Nelson was not structured in inferiority through the operations of the labour market, a fact of immense significance for the position of women in the town. Most employed women worked on more or less equal terms with men and for the same wages. This worked out, in the 1890s, at about 18s. (90p) per week for a four-loom weaver. By the eve of the First World War, pay had risen to around 30s. (£1.50) a week. This represented a rise in wages over that period of more than 60 per cent, which was in excess of the general trend in the Burnley district.[19] In national terms, it was a high level of wage for women, though comparatively low for men. Considering, however, that such wages often contributed to a combined family wage of father/husband, daughter, son, and, frequently, mother/wife, it represented good earnings and gave Nelson weavers in general, and women weavers in particular, a sense of importance and self-confidence. The cultural life of the town – and, to a large extent its politics – acquired a particular distinctiveness as a result of the prominence of women in local industry.

The workforce was also distinctive in another sense. A significant proportion of it was drawn from the employment of children. At the turn of the century, the Lancashire cotton industry employed almost 500,000 people, of whom some 40,000 were children under the age of 14. Of these, approximately 60 per cent were employed as 'half-timers', children, mainly over 12, who gained partial exemption from their schooling in order to work in the mill. Weaving accounted for the majority of them.[20] The system became an increasingly controversial one in the years before the First World War; educationalists were constantly seeking to increase the age of exemption, if not to abolish half-time altogether, whilst cotton-worker parents, employers and trade unions usually combined in defence of the system. Albert Smith, for example, as Labour MP for Clitheroe, defended it vigorously in the House of Commons in 1914. Opposing a clause in the Child Employment and School Attendance Bill which sought to remove local by-law exemptions for half-timers, Smith marshalled a series of arguments in support of the existing system. This included not only the fact that the United Textile Factory Workers had balloted overwhelmingly in support of it, but the assertion that the economic bases of the industry

2.3 Child labour was an important part of cotton weaving, and Nelson had a similar proportion of young people in its labour force to that of other weaving towns. They worked on the 'half-time' principle – attending both school and mill once they had reached the statutory age. In 1899 the age limit for half-time exemption was raised to 12. At this time, there were about 1,000 such workers in Nelson, a number split roughly equally between girls and boys. Parents, employers and cotton trade unions defended the system against educational reformers, mainly on the grounds of the family wage. As one correspondent to the *Nelson Leader* commented in 1914 (8 May): 'If children go to school until they are 14 or 15 how soon will they be able to earn their own living? Certainly not before they are 16 or 17 years, and how are the weaving parents going to make ends meet with a family of children to keep up to 16 before they cease to be a burden?' (*Lancashire Library, Nelson Local Studies Collection*)

would be weakened if half-timers were removed; weavers working on six looms, he claimed, would have to return to four if their young assistants were unavailable, and this would have consequences for both earnings and productivity.[21] Exact figures for the numbers of half-timers in particular districts are difficult to obtain, precisely because of the issue that Smith was debating: the level of educational attainment required before exemption could be claimed varied from one area to another. Census returns, however, give a reasonably sound indication, showing the numbers of both boys and girls employed between the ages of 10–13. From these figures, it is clear that just under 1,000 children in this age group were employed in Nelson at the turn of the century, not all of them, however, in cotton manufacture. This represented approximately 5 per cent of the total employed labour force – 4.3 per cent of the male workforce and 6.5 per cent of the female. This proportion of child labour was much the same as in other Lancashire cotton towns, where on average between 3–4.5 per cent of the male labour force were boys and a slightly higher proportion – around 5.5 per cent to 7.5 per cent – girls.[22] Child labour of this kind was crucially important to parents, contributing to the family economy and helping to sustain the relative prosperity of cotton weavers in the early years of the century.

For all that Nelson weavers possessed a pride in their high-quality product,[23] it should be remembered that weaving was not a skilled trade in the customary sense of the term. It involved neither complex intrinsic skills that commanded a scarcity value in the labour market, nor was its labour supply restricted by the artificial controls over entry into the trade that were to be found, for example, in the male-dominated work of cotton spinning. Weaving was, as H. A. Turner has shown in his study of cotton trade-unionism, an 'open' trade,[24] whatever power its operatives exercised in the labour market resulted largely from the strength of their trade unions.

There were inbuilt disadvantages for labour in the local economy. Nelson's growth had been premised upon the decline of handloom weaving in the surrounding districts and the lack of any significant alternative forms of employment apart from agriculture. Cheap labour was available, therefore, and this was a powerful inducement to capital investment in cotton. Given the absence of any intrinsic skills in weaving, there was always a tendency for wages to be driven down in this type of labour market. What safeguarded labour in the forty or so years before the First World War was the relative buoyancy of local trade and the comprehensive development of trade-union organisation in weaving.

The growth of the Nelson Weavers' Association (NWA), which, by the early years of the twentieth century, had become not only one of the most influential organisations in Nelson itself, but a strong force on cotton politics in Lancashire, has been well told by the Fowlers. Their analysis emphasises the link in the sense of skill and militancy between the handloom weaving tradition and the new organisations of power-loom weavers which provided workers with a strong platform on which to build. Added to this was the fact that a homogeneous workforce and a standardised manufacturing process usually helped to remove some of the obstacles in the way of trade-union recruitment.[25] Furthermore, as Weinroth has pointed out, trade-unionism in Nelson's weaving trade benefited from the absence of an established class of large manufacturers. The proliferation of businesses through the room and power system meant that undercapitalised small producers were generally unable to afford lengthy strikes and tried to settle industrial disputes as quickly as possible. In this context, trade-unionists might have come to feel that militancy paid off, thus explaining the aggressive stance taken on many occasions by the NWA. Its success attracted members, and this accounted for the union's rapid rise.[26]

The earliest trade union to be formed in Nelson (1870) was a branch of the North East Lancashire Weavers' Amalgamation, run by Thomas Birtwistle. Its success was limited and it was not until the formation of

2.4 The Weavers' Institute, opened in 1905, now Silverman Hall. This imposing building was testimony to the power and influence of the Nelson Weavers' Association. At
its peak in the early 1920s, the NWA had some 18,000 members, and the institute
was the hub of the weaver's industrial, political and cultural life. Not only did it
house the offices of the association, but it was the location for regular educational
and cultural events. Such activities were still evident in the early 1960s, but with the
decline of cotton and the consequent drop in trade-union membership, the NWA
found it difficult to meet the costs of maintaining the institute and moved to more
modest premises in Leeds Road. The institute became Silverman Hall in 1968, a social and cultural centre named in honour of Sydney Silverman, MP for Nelson and
Colne from 1935 until his death in 1968.

a second county-wide Weavers' Amalgamation in 1884, of which Nelson
became a district association, that progress began to be made. Personal
factors often explain the success or failure of such developments, and
the appointment of William Ward as secretary in 1886 was an important
landmark in Nelson's case. Ward's efforts in organising the weavers
during the first few years of his post were rewarded by a steady increase
in membership; it had reached around 4,000 by the early 1890s, and
was 6,000 by 1900. Ward's achievements had also prompted the setting-up of a local employers' association by the early 1890s. This helped
to strengthen the bases for collective bargaining on a county-wide front,
the most important outcome of which was the agreement of a uniform
price list in 1892. It established a common standard for weavers' wages
on a county-wide basis. The list provided a uniform method for com-
puting weavers' piece-prices for similar kinds of work in different
districts, thus preventing one group of workers from undercutting
another for the same work. Henceforward, Nelson ceased automatically
to be a low-wage area, though constant vigilance was required on the
part of the NWA to ensure that the application of the uniform list was
honoured by all employers in the district. On the whole it was, before

the First World War. The system began to break down in the 1930s, however, when employers were searching for economies in labour and started to increase the weaver to loom ratio.

The problems of organised labour in an economy like that of Nelson were illustrated in a number of aspects of industrial relations in the late nineteenth and early twentieth century. One issue that provoked widespread anger among weavers was the practice of 'driving' by over-lookers ('tacklers'). This was a method employed by supervisory staff to exact maximum labour power from the weavers, frequently involving the public display of workers' production levels, especially where these were felt to have fallen below expectations. The practice was most often directed by tacklers (always men) against female weavers, and it there-fore had overtones of sexual power. Towards the end of 1891 this issue provoked a major conflict at the firm of Evans and Berry which spilled over into the streets as weavers demonstrated against the importation of blackleg labour to replace workers on strike. The dispute was event-ually settled to the weavers' advantage, but not before an attempt at a compromise by NWA officials had been rejected outright by a mass meeting of union members.[27]

Corporate resistance of this kind was the customary tactic used by the workforce against employers' attempts to install an oppressive labour discipline. In short, the real strength of the workforce lay in its trade-unionism, which explains why membership was high (17,000) and approached a near-total coverage of the weaving population by the years immediately preceding the First World War. The importance of this was demonstrated very clearly in the weaving lockout of 1911–12. This dispute, occasioned by troubles in Accrington, had its origins in general problems of cotton weaving which stretched far beyond the boundaries of Nelson. In Nelson, however, it manifested itself in a unique way, exposing a number of tensions within the local capital–labour relationship. The lockout, both inside Nelson and farther afield, was essentially concerned with the issue of non-unionism. With inflationary pressures mounting on real wages generally in the decade before 1914, the Weavers' Amalgamation responded in 1911 by seeking to reinforce a claim for a wage increase by extending its coverage of the labour force. In effect, the amalgamation went for a 'closed shop' policy in areas where union membership was already high. The strategy backfired, however. The employers' unexpected retaliation with a lock-out snatched the intiative in the dispute and set in motion a sequence of events from which the amalgamation never recovered. The outcome was a defeat for the amalgamation with far-reaching political and industrial consequences which were to haunt the cotton industry in the 1920s.

In the more immediate context of the lockout, Nelson, as Joseph White's study of the dispute has shown,[28] was a focal point of activity.

Here two issues were to the fore. Firstly, the non-union question, which was centred upon a particular local development. In 1906 a trade union based on religious allegiance had been established by a politically aware priest, Father Robert Smith, in reaction to the growing Labour and socialist commitment of the Nelson weavers. The Nelson and District Catholic Workers' Union, as Smith's organisation was known, did not support the 1911–12 lockout, and the activities of its members – less than 200, in comparison with almost 12,000 in the NWA – provoked similar scenes in the streets of Nelson to those that had accompanied the Evans and Berry dispute some twenty years earlier. The continuation of rank-and-file union pressure against members of the Catholic Workers' Union (later renamed the Protection Society) was seen in Nelson long after the Weavers' Amalgamation, with the backing of the leadership of the NWA, had called off the action that had provoked the lockout. During 1913, 'wildcat' strikes were conducted at the Clover, Albert and Brook Street mills by male and female weavers determined to stamp out the rival union. As a tactic, this grass-roots action was successful, for the Protection Society appears to have folded during the course of the year and some of its leading members rejoined the NWA.[29]

It was to be expected that Nelson workers would commit themselves to a struggle over non-unionism. What is equally significant, though less prominent, in these disputes, however, is the second issue revealed by the events: rank-and-file workers' initiative. Though the officials of the NWA remained in overall control of union policy, there were times when their position was more a response to membership opinion than an attempt to lead it. This became apparent during the wildcat strikes of 1913. At no point were these part of formal NWA policy. Though White suggests that the strikes had the tacit approval of NWA officials,[30] there is little doubt that Nelson weavers were in no mood to be dictated to by either employers or union leaders. Clearly, the climate of industrial relations in the town had encouraged a fiercely militant outlook on the part of many weavers.

On the whole, though, conflict of this nature was not the norm in the pre-war period. The nature of their product and its market meant that Nelson employers and workers could expect to have their share of economic prosperity – to the extent, that is, that the unregulated pre-war economy allowed anyone to escape the sequence of boom and slump that seemed to be almost as natural as the weather. Good trade could turn to bad remarkably quickly. The *Nelson Leader*, for example, reviewing the cotton trade at the beginning of 1914, contrasted the 'exceptional prosperity and expansion' that had been experienced in 1912 with the bad year that followed.[31] In these fluctuating conditions, employers and workers had become accustomed to a conventional response to bad trade which took the form of short-time working. Mills would shut down for part of the week – or, in some cases, stop altogether

– until demand had righted. To compensate companies experiencing such difficulties, the Nelson employers developed a scheme in 1909 whereby a levy of 1s. (5p) was made on all the looms in the district to create a fund from which companies on short time could be subsidised. Attempts to regulate the local economy in this way were limited, however. Since the sudden emergence of Nelson's cotton trade in the 1870s, there had been more good years than bad and, in the main, it did not seem necessary to implement any overarching control of the industry. The notion of 'prosperity' would not be too wide of the mark if applied to the town during these years. As the Fowlers note: 'there is no better indicator of this prosperity than the annual exodus to Blackpool at Wakes Week when the town was deserted'.[32] The pre-war economy was a far from ideal way of organising work and business, but, seen against some of the dismal prospects of trade disruption and unemployment that loomed large on the outbreak of war in August 1914, it appeared to have advantages.[33] Compared with what followed on many occasions after 1918, this pre-war period resembled utopia.

The Making of a Borough, 1864–1914

Welcome! Welcome! to the Charter, Granted now to Nelson town; 'Mong new boroughs none is smarter Than the place we proudly own:– Onward toiling, ever thriving, Fame she'd win, and wealth attain, In the paths of duty striving – England's hero o'er again![1]

Rarely was the influence of Nelson's small middle class more prominently in evidence than in the events surrounding the granting of the town's Charter of Incorporation in 1890. In July of that year Nelson achieved municipal borough status. On a sunny day at the end of August the town celebrated its achievement with a display of pageantry and civic consciousness that was unique in its history. An estimated 80,000 people poured into Nelson to enjoy the festivities. Public buildings, shops and private houses were bedecked with bunting and mottoes ('Nelson expects every man to do his duty', proclaimed the one over the Market Hall); the main roads were each provided with triumphal arches, erected from subscriptions made by tradespeople; and at the junction of Market Street and Manchester Road, at the very centre of the town, a castellated arch representing an ancient gateway had been constructed. The centre-piece of the day's events was what the *Nelson Chronicle* described as a 'monstre [*sic*] procession', which headed off along Manchester Road just after 3pm and followed a roughly clockwise route through the main streets of the town. It was led by a troop of mounted policemen and contained sections of all the major groups within the town – Sunday schools (represented by some 8,000 scholars), the Corporation itself (in the form of its various departments, whose work was depicted on 'lurries' bearing tableaux), the Post Office, the St John Ambulance Brigade, the Co-operative Society, the East Lancashire Volunteer Regiment, the Fire Brigade, four friendly societies, and a long procession of floats representing various trades. The last sections of the procession were just starting out when the leaders reappeared, over an hour after their departure. Thereafter, the focal point of activity was the area around the Town Hall, where crowds gathered to hear the reading of the charter and speeches by some of the local celebrities whose efforts had brought about the town's new-found

3.1 Charter Day, 30 August 1890, without question the grandest event staged in Nelson to that date, and possibly since. The *Nelson Chronicle* estimated that 80,000 people were in the town that day. The granting of borough status was seen as a prelude to the further growth of the town, an understandable feeling in view of its spectacular rise over the previous 20 years: 'Nelson has few parallels in its singular rise from a small to an important place' (*Nelson Chronicle*, 18 April 1890). In fact, however, the town was nearing the peak of its growth by this stage. (*Lancashire Library, Nelson Local Studies Collection*)

status. In the evening, Nelson was ablaze with a multiplicity of electric and gas lights. The day ended with a firework display at the recreation ground, from which there had previously been despatched 'montgolfiers and grotesque shaped balloons'. 'Thousands upon thousands of people witnessed the display of fireworks, and the crush was great.'[2]

Events of this kind were not uncommon in towns which had received incorporated status. In the new town of Nelson, however, they took on a special significance. Not only did they proclaim a constitututional elevation, inaugurating a new era of local government; for Nelsonians they also served to register the existence of a community. Charter Day celebrated both the making of Nelson and the making of Nelsonians. The procession, for example, was a symbolic representation not only of the town's various trades, but also of their mutual interdependence and unity. Moreover, the prominent role given to certain notables, both in the way in which the celebrations foregrounded them and in the manner in which the local press wrote up its record of Charter Day, was very clearly designed to identify a group of leaders whose energies had helped to create modern Nelson and who were, in a very real sense, the embodiment of the town. In all these ways, the day was an important civic event for a town like Nelson. Its very lack of history and traditions made the creation of an 'invented' tradition, with its triumphal arches and Sunday scholars dressed in 'historic' garb, the more necessary. On 30 August 1890 Nelson was, to some extent, inventing itself as a community, projecting its short but dynamic growth onto a future that would be yet more prosperous.

This idealisation of the town masked the political realities of the situation. Borough status was the outcome of a process of lobbying by local businessmen for the powers that the charter endowed. In the course of the previous 25 years, Nelson and its surrounding districts had acquired a well-defined (though, in general, financially moderately endowed) élite of political and social leaders whose chief aim by the late 1880s was to transform the existing form of local government – the Local Board – into a fully-fledged borough corporation. This objective had a particular purpose in Nelson because of the nature of land and property ownership in the area. As we saw in the previous chapter, the cotton industry was characterised by a profusion of small businesses. In the mid-1880s, for example, 70 per cent of Nelson's manufacturing companies operated between 100 and 500 looms. Only three concerns were able to operate more than 1,000 looms. Likewise, there were no dominant landowners and farmers. This fact was plainly demonstrated in the Tithe Award of 1842, which apportioned rent charges in lieu of tithes, for the townships of Great and Little Marsden. It reveals a proliferation of small property holders and occupiers, the vast majority of whom possessed less than 50 acres. The exceptions were John Ridehalgh (c. 250 acres), Charles Towneley (300 acres), Robert Towneley-Parker (c. 320 acres), W. L. Sagar (220 acres), and Matthew Walton (c. 600 acres). These landowners, most of whose property was tenanted in small acreages, were relatively small by national standards. None of them, neither the 'pre-industrial' landowners nor the later industrialists, possessed the economic resources which would have been needed if they were to shape the town's development through the exercise of independent patronage.[3]

Indeed, in economic terms, there were only two figures who could be considered 'giants': William Farrer Ecroyd, who headed the Ecroyd family business at Lomeshaye following the death of his father in 1876; and William Tunstill of Reedyford Hall, who manufactured at both Brierfield, where he was by far the dominant employer, and Nelson. Each was untypical of the business élite in many ways. The Ecroyds, for example, had a much longer association with the district than any other manufacturers, going back to the sixteenth century. Moreover, they were noted for their woollen, not cotton, goods. They had originally been a Quaker family, but by the late nineteenth century

3.2 William Tunstill, described by one writer as 'Nelson's Rockefeller', was the district's leading figure alongside W. F. Ecroyd in the years between the 1870s and the turn of the century. The Tunstills were a local family who owned mills in both Nelson and Brierfield. William Tunstill, a leading support of Wesleyan Methodism, had been active in local politics in the 1870s, but by the 1890s had extended his business interests into a regional and national arena and, therefore, tended to withdraw from direct involvement in the political life of Nelson.

W. F. Ecroyd had moved to Anglicanism and had become a patron of both the Church of England and the Conservative Party, which set the family apart from the dominant religious and political temper of the locality. Both families were also singular in terms of the patronage they were able to mobilise on behalf of Nelson. The Ecroyds were noted for their paternalism; they had built a model village for their workers at Lomeshaye, where there was also a factory school. William Tunstill directed much of the profits of his business into Wesleyan Methodism, providing many of the funds needed for a flurry of building activity in the 1890s which saw the creation of the Fleet Street, Temple Street and Bradley Hall chapels. But the immediate district was only one sphere of their economic and political activities. W. F. Ecroyd served as MP for Preston in the 1870s, marking him out as part of a regional, if not a national, middle class. William Tunstill, a JP like Ecroyd, also moved in broader circles than other Nelson businessmen. Though he continued to be involved in the religious and political life of Nelson as a Wesleyan and a Liberal, his business dealings had secured him a

3.3 Lomeshaye House, home of the Ecroyds, one of Nelson's old established proper-tied families. By the late seventeenth century they were installed at Edge End in Little Marsden, where a textile business was begun towards the middle of the eighteenth century. By the 1770s it had been transferred to Lomeshaye, where William Ecroyd set up a mill colony on the banks of Pendle Water. The company specialised in high-quality woollen cloths, winning a gold medal at the Great Exhibition of 1851, but suffered after the First World War and was sold off in 1934. William Farrer Ecroyd headed the business in the late nineteenth century. He was Conservative in politics and, although the family had a Quaker history, a supporter of the Church of England, being a particular patron of St Mary's Church. (*Lancashire Library, Nelson Local Studies Collection*)

directorship of a regional bank, a coal company, and the position of vice-chairman of the Lancashire and Yorkshire Railway. He has been described as 'Nelson's Rockefeller'.[4] By the 1880s his days as an active participant in the local struggle for power and influence were behind him. Like Ecroyd, he had served as chairman of the Nelson Local Board in its early days, but as his interests grew and his contacts widened, he was able to leave this sphere of operations to smaller men. He continued, until his death in 1903, to live at Reedyford Hall on the outskirts of Nelson, but his role increasingly was that of a benevolent but distant patrician.[5]

In the 1870s, however, Ecroyd and Tunstill had been part of a group of local businessmen who controlled Nelson politics. Their power base was the Nelson Local Board. This institution was an assemblage of ratepayers' representatives that was formed in 1864 under the terms of the 1848 Public Health Act and the 1858 Local Government Act. This legislation had enabled local ratepayers to petition for powers, in the form of a Local Board of Health, to deal with a range of public health issues, including sewerage, drainage, water supply, the management of streets and burial grounds. The board was empowered to levy district rates based on Poor Law assessments. Voting rights were related to the rateable value of property, which meant that wealthy residents might accrue up to 12 votes in board elections. Candidates for membership, in areas with a population of less than 20,000, had to hold property with a rateable value of at least £15, or personal property with a value of £500 or more.

Proposals to establish a board in the Marsden district met, as Bennett has shown,[6] with the broad support of the manufacturing interest. The farmers generally opposed it, feeling that the change would increase rates without bringing any tangible benefits to the outlying districts. Their opposition ensured that a poll of ratepayers was necessary before further moves could be made. The poll of October 1864, conducted in a spirit of some excitement, produced a decisive vote in favour of constituting a Local Board – 430 votes to 221. The new Board covered the parish of Little Marsden and the greater part of Great Marsden, encompassing a population of some 3,500. Its first meeting, chaired by William Tunstill, was held the very day after the declaration of the poll, and this enthusiastic beginning to its life was maintained thereafter.

Nelson's Local Board could, and frequently did, point to an impressive record of achievement during its 26 years of existence. One of the themes of the speeches on Charter Day was the opportunity that the town's new status afforded for continuing and augmenting the foundations of civic government already laid by the Local Board. There was more than an echo in the *Nelson Chronicle*'s appraisal of the work of the Local Board of Joseph Chamberlain's celebrated claims for municipal reform in Birmingham in the 1870s. Among the provisions listed were: gas, market, library, parks, street paving, and general sanitation.[7] What is more, many of these ventures – launched with capital either levied through the rates or borrowed – had proved commercially successful. The gasworks, for example, purchased by the Local Board in 1866, was showing an annual profit of some £3,500 by the late 1880s. Nelson's water supply, a perennial source of comment because of the needs of a growing population and the demands of the cotton industry, was drawn from reservoirs constructed by the Local Board and was also made available for sale to the urban districts of Brierfield and Barrowford.

This municipal thrust is not surprising considering the composition of the Local Board. Its members were essentially small businessmen whose own resources were insufficient to provide any foundation for a paternalist style of local government. Nelson's long history of public initiative in this field began with the Local Board in the 1860s and reached its peak with the municipal socialism of the Labour Party in the interwar years. In the absence of any local grandee whose economic strength might provide voluntary cultural and welfare services, the borough looked to itself to service the perceived needs of the town.

The character of this local leadership was neatly embodied in the men who made up the Incorporation Committee, a group set up by the Local Board to lobby for charter status. There were four elected members of the Local Board – Samuel Gott, William Hartley, William Astley and John Wilkinson – together with the town clerk, R. M. Prescott. Each individual's history reflected in some measure the development of Nelson. Only Hartley was a native of the district, the others being immigrants – Prescott from St Helens, and Gott, Astley and Wilkinson all from that Lancashire–Yorkshire borderland area that provided so many of Nelson's early migrants. All had quite humble origins and were 'self-made' men, though Astley had benefited from inheriting his father's business in Clitheroe. Wilkinson and Hartley were both cotton manufacturers. Astley, though better known as the owner of Nelson Brewery, was a director of seven room and power companies. Gott, the oldest member of the group and the man designated as Nelson's first mayor, represented the 'shopocracy' in his trade as a draper. In politics, the general proclivity was for Liberalism, buttressed by Nonconformity in religion. Astley was the exception in this case; like most brewers, he sided with the Conservatives. All had served as chairmen of the Local Board in addition to having worked on important committees. Hartley in particular had been instrumental in negotiations to extend water supplies by the acquisition of a reservoir in the Ogden valley, a scheme completed in 1890. The town clerk, Prescott, had risen most rapidly of all. After holding a succession of posts in local government in various Lancashire towns, he was appointed to the Nelson position in 1888 while still under the age of 30. He later went on to become town clerk of Sheffield, though he died relatively young in 1913. They were, according to the *Nelson Chronicle*, 'a circle of self-made men of whose success Nelson has today every reason to be alike grateful and proud'.[8]

Men like these had taken the lead in Nelson politics in the 1880s. The idea of incorporation was a compelling one for them. As the local press was fond of reminding its readers, the town's rise and prosperity were closely linked to the initiatives of such people – not only as a result of their business acumen, but because their efforts in providing good sanitation and general services through the Local Board had been a crucial element in attracting capital and labour to the town. It seemed likely, therefore, that continuing progress on this front would ensure continuing business activity: 'Incorporation is no final goal, not even a half-way house, but a post-station on the way of social, moral and material progress.'[9] As a Local Board, however, the extent of both their borrowing power and their sanctioning of loans was limited by the monitoring role of the Local Government Board, a government department in London. It was this feeling of circumscription in respect of future development that prompted the *Nelson Chronicle* to launch a campaign for a charter in 1887. Municipal borough status would certainly bring greater financial independence, not only through the power to set a borough rate, but also to borrow money for urban development on the security of that rate and of other corporate assets such as land and property. Support for incorporation was also given by the House of Commons Police and Sanitary Regulations Committee, which had scrutinised the Nelson Local Government Bill in 1888 which sought sanction to spend some £300,000 on gas and water improvements. It was felt in Parliament that the incorporation of the borough should be the logical outcome of this activity.[10] Local opinion on the matter grew quickly, and by October 1889 a petition had been submitted to the Privy Council.

A further consideration which lent some weight to the idea of borough status stemmed from the concern over ground values. As John Wilkinson pointed out in proposing the toast 'To the Town and Trade of Nelson' at the banquet on Charter Day, the manufacturing capacity, population and rateable value of property in the town had all increased significantly over the previous quarter century: 'the number of looms had multiplied seven times, and the rateable value had gone up fourteen times'.[11] To many in his audience, the conclusion to be drawn from this statement of facts was inescapable: the increase in trade was inextricably linked to the increasing value of property, some of which was the very land upon which property was built. To secure the future growth of trade and property values, the town needed to build the foundations of municipal services which would attract both trade and people to it. To achieve this, however, there needed to be a tax on that group of people who had benefited in terms of property values without necessarily having made a financial contribution: the ground landlords. 'It is only fair and just', the *Nelson Chronicle* had argued earlier, 'that the landlords whose property derives augmented value should bear a proper proportion of the cost.'[12] The taxation of land had been a persistent theme in Liberal thinking since the days of the Corn Laws. By the 1880s, with the onset of national economic problems resulting from the trade depression that had started in the previous decade, the idea of taxing land was developing in new directions. Land nationalisation was one proposal to emerge. So, too, was the idea of the 'single tax' (that is, on land) popularised by the American Henry George in his book *Progress and Poverty* (1879). Municipal boroughs were not free to introduce such ideas themselves, but the opportunities afforded by council rates helped to shore up the financial difficulties of local government, against the day when a national (probably Liberal) government might introduce a radical fiscal measure to grapple properly with the country's economic problems. A new borough council like that of Nelson, its esteem enhanced by its elevation, could add its political weight to the pressure for change. However, the principle of municipal intervention to provide for the well-being of inhabitants – and the public spending that was an inevitable accompaniment to it – was already established in Nelson in 1890. It was a principle that was to form a dominant motif in the subsequent history of the borough.

It is, however, one thing to mark the creation of a borough by the granting of a charter; it is quite another matter to create the unity of people that the Corporation officially represents. How far did Nelson, in the years before the First World War, succeed in becoming a viable entity in which the inevitable diversity of a rapidly formed urban community was nonetheless given coherence by a sense of civic unity? New towns, even planned ones, are not always successful as places in which to live. Nelson was not planned. In fact, Jill Liddington has gone so far as to liken Nelson and Brierfield at this time to 'frontier towns of the American west'.[13] In addition to newness and the inflow of migrants, the image suggests a certain tension within the community. In the absence of any strong paternalist control, it might be considered a valid image for Nelson. The example of nearby Burnley lends credibility to it. Though a larger town (its population was approaching 100,000 by the 1890s) which evolved at a slightly earlier stage, Burnley nevertheless shared the feature of rapid development with Nelson. By the 1870s this had brought its share of housing and health problems, especially infant mortality, and the place had become something of a byword for crime and drunkenness. Although improvements were being made by the turn of the century, Burnley did not present an attractive proposition, especially to visitors. The socialist politician H. M. Hyndman, who visited the town on several occasions and stood for Parliament there four times between 1895 and 1910, had a low opinion of the place. On one occasion he commented: 'a beautiful valley has been completely spoiled by one of the most ungainly and smoky manufacturing towns which it is possible to set eyes upon'. On another he advised a friend – 'if you are thinking of visiting Burnley – don't'.[14]

Nelson escaped many of these problems. Its size and compactness were advantageous, as was the proportion of owner-occupiers in the town. From the earliest stages of growth in the 1860s and 1870s, when over 2,000 houses were built using stone from local quarries and were laid out in an orderly pattern, Nelson always maintained a reputation for a small amount of slum property and a generally good standard of housing, with probably half of the 10,000 houses by 1914 being privately bought with building society mortgages.[15] The layout of the town and its housing made it, as one commentator has noted, 'easy to police'.[16]. This should be taken to mean that not only did the County Constabulary, with a force of 40 officers led by an inspector in 1914, experience fewer problems in Nelson than in some other areas of Lancashire, but that the compact neighbourhoods policed themselves. In other words, there was a social as well as a legal form of control at work.

This becomes evident when we consider one of the chief features of Nelson's social life in the late nineteenth century. Perhaps the most important factor shaping the town's early social development was immigration. Several studies of immigrants in various locations have concluded that they keep together in their new environments, often for many years.[17] The popular idea of assimilation, of locals and immigrants fusing together in a 'melting pot' of culture, needs to be treated with caution. Immigrant communities usually cluster around institutions that have either been imported with them or which, like Methodism, are part of a wider network to be found both at points of departure and of arrival. Such institutions provide a source of togetherness and identity for migrants, but, at the same time, they serve to keep them apart from the indigenous population. Some of these characteristics were present in Nelson, but, because many of the inhabitants were immigrants to a greater or lesser extent, there was none of the bitterness and occasional violence that existed where a significant group of immigrants was confronted by a large and resentful native population. This happened in many parts of Lancashire in the second half of the nineteenth century as a result of Irish Catholic migration, which shaped the region's politics and culture in a profound way. Little of this occurred in Nelson, but immigrant culture was pronounced and, therefore, it is probably more realistic to regard the town not so much as a single community, but as a collection of different ones, each clustered around a particular focal point.

One of these was undoubtedly the chapel. By the end of the century a wide range of denominations was present in the town. Wesleyan Methodism, with six places of worship in Nelson alone, was the most prominent. The movement had sunk firm roots in the area since the early nineteenth century. Its position in Nelson owed much, as we have seen, to the patronage of William Tunstill, who had not only acted as a benefactor but had also served as the movement's local treasurer. Wesleyanism's nerve-centre was the Carr Road chapel, built in 1863 with 800 places. Evidence of the Wesleyans' continuing influence in the town was the chapel in Railway Street, opened in 1890 and capable of seating 1,200 worshippers. Other branches of Methodism were also present, some of a more demotic nature than Wesleyanism. The United Methodists and the Primitive Methodists, always associated with working men and women, were both active, as were the older dissenting sects of Baptists and Congregationalists. It was the Baptists, from their Zion Chapel in Elizabeth Street, who were responsible for creating one of Nelson's best-known institutions, the prize-winning Nelson Excelsior Prize Glee Union. The Salvation Army further supplemented the nonconformist ranks, which showed its

3.4 The Nelson Excelsior Glee Union, a choral group which had originated at the Zion Baptist Chapel in Elizabeth Street before the First World War. Choral singing had a strong following in Nelson, and its choirs were prominent in national competitions. One of the leading exponents of the art was the Arion Glee Union, which won a first prize at the Welsh National Eisteddfod in 1919 and performed with celebrities such as the Lancashire tenor Tom Bourke. (*Lancashire Library, Nelson Local Studies Collection*)

potential for yet further growth in the years just before the First World War with the blossomimg of the Ebenezer Chapel, established by the Central Gospel Mission following an initial missionary venture to Barrowford by the London-based Central Evangelisation Society in the early years of the century. Ebenezer Chapel had a lively programme of religious activities which included mothers' classes, choirs, an orchestra and a Sunshine Band, which regularly visited the sick and needy – all in addition to normal religious services.[18] Two other distinctive groups were of a very much more local origin: the Inghamites, with a chapel in Russell Street which the manufacturer James Nelson attended, comprised a small body found only in this part of Lancashire; and the Independent Methodists, who exercised a strong influence in Nelson, one of their main centres in a network of chapels which extended only over the north-west of England.

The Independent Methodists illustrate the concept of a religious community very clearly. Their chapel, Salem, with a capacity of 900 places close to the town centre, was a hub of theological and political activity which gave the sect a high profile in Nelson. Unlike the Wesleyans, they had no close connection with local manufacturers, nor did they operate a system of pew renting for wealthy members of their congregation. Their egalitarian spirit was evinced in the manner of their origins, as a breakaway sect from the Primitive Methodists in the 1850s,

3.5 Salem Chapel, headquarters of the Independent Methodists, a small movement nationally but very active and influential in Nelson. Salem was the hub of a dynamic and democratic religious community which sustained a range of activities, in which education and politics were prominent. The Independent Methodists prided them-selves on their continuing contribution to the political life of Nelson and could usually point to the presence of some of their members on the Town Council. Salem boasted almost 1,000 Sunday school pupils in the early years of this century. The chapel itself was the largest in Nelson, with 900 places. (*Lancashire Library, Nelson Local Studies Collection*)

when a small congregation installed itself in humble premises known as the 'Dandy Shop' at Bradley Lane Head. Egalitarian, too, was the structure of chapel governance that they adopted, with its commitment to democracy, unpaid ministers and voting equality between men and women. They recognised no religious titles or designations. They were strongly evangelical in religious practice, fiercely in favour of temperance and opposed to the Established Church. The spirit of the Independent Methodists was enshrined in their educational work, which extended beyond a very active Sunday school (some 1,000 scholars by the turn of the century) to a daytime provision which became a leading element of Nelson's school system in the late nineteenth century. In the 1920s the organisation even opened a new school on the profits of a sale of land to Montague Burton for a new shop. Youth was always an essential feature of the Independent Methodists. They formed a dynamic group who made a distinctive and progressive political contribution to Nelson and who could usually point to the representation of their members on the Town Council.[19] In many ways, therefore, their organisation and beliefs were a distillation of the outlook of the Lancashire and Yorkshire uplands, whose independent-minded farmers and weavers had taken the road to Nelson. They were typified in the Carradice brothers – Dan, William and Harrison – from Kirkby Malham in the Yorkshire Dales, who were keen members of the Salem Chapel before gravitating into socialist politics and becoming leading figures in the Independent Labour Party (ILP).[20]

By contrast, the Church of England, though well represented by places of worship, was less actively supported. By the beginning of the twentieth century there were four Anglican churches in Nelson. Apart from St Paul's in Little Marsden, which dated from the thirteenth century and had been rebuilt early in the nineteenth, all had come into existence since the growth of Nelson. St Mary's in Manchester Road was started in 1877 with money and land provided by W. F. Ecroyd and was finished in 1908. Just before this, in 1902, St Philip's in Leeds Road had been consecrated. By this time St John's had been restored and St Paul's was about to be renovated. Each church was within reach of working-class neighbourhoods and offered a high number of free sittings; indeed, only St Philip's retained a system of pew rents. These attempts by the Anglicans to keep pace with nonconformist development show a vigorous and well-funded community, though ultimately one that lacked popular appeal.[21]

Roman Catholicism was provided for by five establishments. Little of the English tradition of Catholicism, so evident in Preston, appears to have existed in Nelson. Most Catholic activity dates from the 1870s, when priests took up residence in Colne. The first foray into Nelson came in 1883 with the establishment of a mission in Every Street; thereafter, churches and chapels were set up regularly until just before the First World War. This late growth is explained by immigration, in this case of Irish people moving into Nelson from other Lancashire towns rather than directly from Ireland. A census of religious attendance conducted by the Salford Catholic diocese around the turn of the century suggests that there were about 1,500 communicants in Nelson. Though not large in numbers, the Catholic community was an influential one in Nelson. It was especially active in education, with an impressive school-building programme in the 1890s, and commanded an important following in politics. The United Irish League, with Patrick Quinn one of its leading members, was an important ally of

3.6 St Mary the Virgin, the largest of the four Anglican churches in a strongly noncon-formist town. Building was started in the 1870s with money and land donated by W. F. Ecroyd, who laid the foundation stone. The architects were the Burnley firm of Waddingtons, who designed a number of public buildings throughout Lancashire at this time. A style derived from the thirteenth century was chosen in an attempt to give this new town an appearance of medievalism. The church was consecrated in 1879 by Bishop Fraser of Manchester. Building was finally completed in 1908. In an effort to compete with the various nonconformist chapels, the Church of England dis-pensed with the system of pew rents in all but one (St Philip's) of its churches in Nelson. St Mary's had 750 places, all free. (*Lancashire Library, Nelson Local Studies Collection*)

the Labour Party in the years immediately after the First World War, though not by any means a subservient one. Labour supporters like Selina Cooper and her friends in the ILP found that over issues such as birth control, which was beginning to generate public discussion in the 1920s, the Catholic Irish community would refuse its assistance and would stand firm to its own principles.[22]

The religious community, then, was fragmented into a series of competing and occasionally opposed interests and allegiances. Each had its own distinctive culture, derived not simply from the theological position of the group, but also from its political and social activities. Chapel communities provided a way of life for their members. Temperance, for example, was a paramount social concern for all nonconformist denominations, which helps to explain the relative absence of drunkenness in the town. John Walton has pointed out that the comparatively small number of public houses reflected the timing of Nelson's growth, which had taken place after the tightening-up of licensing regulations in the late 1860s and early 1870s,[23] when magistrates (often, like William Tunstill, drawn from the nonconformist community) had greater powers to refuse and suppress licenses. A further important element in this way of life was the attention given to education. The provision of schools was seen as a crucial part of religious activity. A measure of the success with which the denominations pursued this objective in Nelson was the fact that, until 1892, the town possessed no School Board. Allowance for this had been made in the Education Act of 1870 – and Barrowford had set one up as early as 1874 – but voluntary provision removed the need for one in Nelson.[24] Two board schools came into being during the 1890s, but, by the end of the decade, the voluntary establishments, with over 3,000 pupils, took twice as many children.[25] Sunday schools crucially reinforced this activity, as the pride of place given to the 8,400 scholars in the procesion on Charter Day bore witness to.

By this time, other focal points of allegiance were beginning to develop. Religion, though still important, was no longer the dominant cultural force that it had been 30 years earlier. In secular terms, a powerful cluster of interests began to develop around the Weavers' Institute, which opened in Pendle Street in 1905. Social class and labour solidarity constituted the bond that drew people together here. The primary purpose of the Weavers' Institute was to orchestrate the activities of the Nelson Weavers' Association, a trade union with over 6,000 members by the early years of the century. But it also acted as a social and cultural centre where meetings on a range of political and industrial issues were held, inevitably drawing a strong socialist interest. In fact, the offices of the Weavers' Association (in pre-institute days) had been the venue for the meeting which formed the Independent Labour Party in Nelson in 1892. Separate in origin from the Weavers' Association, though increasingly closely linked politically by the early years of the twentieth century, was the Nelson Co-operative and Industrial Society. Its history went back to 1860, when it was set up, according to later accounts, in the weft room at Ecroyd's Lomeshaye Mill, possibly at the instigation of William Ecroyd himself, always keen that his workers should engage in morally improving pursuits. After a shaky start, it had grown into an extensive retail operation by the late 1860s, encompassing drapery, boots and shoes, and groceries. By the 1890s 'industrial' de-partments such as painting and decorating, plumbing, cabinet-making and joinery had been added, together with the ownership of cotton mills and two farms at Barrowford. By 1914 the Co-op was by far the largest retail business in the town, with 24 separate departments. True to its origins, though, it was more than simply a range of shops. The Co-op could justifiably claim to be a community. Its members, of which there were some 7,000 in the district by the mid-1890s (a considerable proportion of a total population of just over 30,000), not only shared in the profits of the business, through the famous 'divi', but were provided with a cultural focus to their lives in the form of a reading-room, a free library and a savings bank. The Educational Department was especially active in organising lectures, concerts, tea parties and billiards. It also claimed to have been 'largely instrumental in refining the musical tastes of the town'.[26]

In all of these communities, the sexes mixed fairly freely. Nelson was spared the rigid sexual divisions of labour and leisure that were to be found in Victorian society more generally. What was a source of division in other towns – men and women neither worked nor played together – was less marked in Nelson. The relative openness of weaving, in gender terms, goes a long way towards explaining this state of affairs. It enabled women to work on roughly equal terms with men and was not seen as exclusively 'women's work'. Women's contribution to the economy as wage-earners was recognised and valued. Moreover, women were able to work at the mills after marriage, which meant that family life developed in a less paternalist fashion, with men prepared to take on some of the domestic duties. All this gave Nelsonian women a certain self-confidence not always seen elsewhere, encouraging them to participate in the life of the community. Their role in the industrial struggles of 1911–13, for example, was often crucial. So it was, too, in another area of life usually regarded as a male preserve: politics. Jill Liddington's biography of Selina Cooper shows her to have been one of the most dynamic figures in the political life of Nelson over a period of 50 years, when a strong current of feminism was present in the town's political culture. The Women's Co-operative Guild, one of the bodies which served to initiate Mrs Cooper into politics, was an active force, as was the socialist movement later, with its ability to attract persuasive national speakers to the area. Both were influential

3.7 Nelson Public Library. A symmetrical architectural style befitted a building dedi-
cated to a balanced mind. Free library provision had been available in Nelson since
1890, but this new building was opened in February 1908 as part of a small precinct
of municipal premises which included a town hall, a technical school and a fire
station. None of them aspired to the architectural grandeur seen in larger provincial
towns, but the library, though not the most conspicuous, was perhaps the most
imaginative of Nelson's public buildings. It was designed by J. R. Poyser and W. B.
Savidge in a baroque style, 'but not too frolicsome', according to the architectural historian Nikolaus Pevsner. A local description shortly after the library's opening declared
it to be a 'distinct ornament to the neighbourhood'.

in placing women's issues on the political platform. Subjects such as
birth control and votes for women were part of the local contribution
to the 'revolt of the daughters' which was emerging nationally at this
time.[27] Women, single and married, buoyed by the relative gender
equality of Nelson, were seeking to consolidate and extend their quality
of life.

The existence of these separate communities gave Nelson a rich
cultural diversity in the pre-war era, but the effects of this should not
be overemphasised. In the years after 1890 a number of developments
were giving substance to a civic identity which welded some of the
separate elements together. 'Nelson' was becoming more than simply
a place where people lived. For one thing, the Corporation itself was
beginning to acquire a physical persona. Its clearest manifestation came
in the form of a collection of public buildings, most of which were
erected after 1890. Work on the Town Hall was started in 1882, with
enlargements after 1890 (and further extensions in the 1930s); a

municipal park was laid out between 1888 and 1897; a market hall
opened in 1889; the Municipal Technical School in 1895; the Public
Library was greatly embellished in 1908; and new public baths opened
in 1913. If these buildings proclaimed a corporate idea of Nelson, they
also signified the provision of an important range of public services.
Since the early days of the Local Board, Nelsonians had been accustomed to the efficient provision of health-related services, with water
supply a constant priority. With incorporation, the new Town Council
became associated with a wider and improved range of services, though
most of these public activities had actually been initiated in the closing
days of the Local Board. New developments after 1890 included the
building of the new library and public baths, the opening of a smallpox
hospital at Catlow in 1902, when an electric light and power works
was also completed, and the assumption, following the Education Act
of 1902 and the disbanding of the School Boards, of responsibility for
elementary education. It was mainly after the war that the Council's
role in public services expanded significantly, especially in the areas of
housing and welfare. However, the provision of public services was
scarcely more important than the big political breakthrough that incorporation represented. Henceforward (following the Municipal
Corporations Act of 1882), any ratepayer could be nominated for
election to the Council. More important still, those elections were now
to be virtually on the principle of one man, one vote. Indeed, women,
if ratepayers, were also eligible to vote in Council elections. Nelson's
local government could therefore be considered to be in the hands of
the people of Nelson; if not quite all the people (receipt of poor relief,
for example, was a disqualification), then almost all, and certainly a
significantly larger number than at any time in the past.[28]

Alongside these changes in the governance of the borough, a host
of other institutions could claim to be expressing the idea of Nelson;
for example, the weekly newspaper the *Nelson Leader*, owned by the
Coulton family and dating from the early 1890s, from which time it
rivalled and eventually supplanted older titles such as the *Colne and
Nelson Times* and the *Nelson Chronicle*. Though Liberal in inclination,
the *Leader* never placed party before town. Nelson Cricket Club, formed
in the 1860s and already known throughout Lancashire by the early
1890s for the skill of its players (Joe Hulme and Willis Cuttell in
particular), was another institution by which Nelson's name spread
abroad. The various musical clubs fulfilled a similar function; the Arion
Glee Union was a leading performer, capable of taking a first prize at
the Welsh National Eisteddfod in 1919. It was seen by the *Leader* as
offering a forum where 'all classes can meet on one common platform,
in the pursuit of the same ideal'.[29] The Reedyford Memorial Hospital
became a focus of local patriotism, in the inter-war years, the subject
of constant fund-raising activities which had raised over £20,000 by

3.8 James Nelson's ('Jimmy Nelson's') sports club, adjacent to the company's mills in the area of Southfield Street. Nelson's had become the largest employer in the town by the eve of the First World War. The sports club, built in the 1920s as a memorial to workers killed in the war, is a fine example of industrial paternalism and welfare in a town where such initiatives were rare. (*Lancashire Library, Nelson Local Studies Collection*)

1934 and made possible the building of a new hospital in 1935. Established in 1920 in memory of Nelsonians who had lost their lives in the First World War, Reedyford Hospital was in many ways also a memorial of the town's development. It had been the home of William Tunstill before the war, but was converted to an auxiliary hospital in 1915. It was eventually bought by the Corporation, thereby following the path from private to public that was so typical of Nelson's community life.

In many towns of a similar size, civic consciousness might have been embodied in a leading public figure. Lancaster, for example, possessed its local seigneur in the form of James Williamson, later Lord Ashton, a linoleum manufacturer and major employer whose benevolence found expression in the endowment of schools, hospitals, a library, an impressive town hall and a park to which he gave his name. No one emerged on a similar scale in Nelson. James Nelson and, more especially his son Amos, who was knighted in 1922, were the leading employers in cotton by the eve of the First World War. Amos Nelson bestowed generous sports facilities to his employees at Valley Mills in the 1920s, but this patronage was limited to his own workforce. His name never became synonymous with Nelson (except, of course, in the literal sense) in the way that Williamson's did with Lancaster. It is interesting to

note that in the general election of 1923 Sir Amos Nelson, who had
served as mayor of the town before the war, was persuaded by the
Conservatives to contest the Nelson and Colne seat against Arthur
Greenwood, Labour, and J. H. S. Aitken, Liberal. Both Aitken and
Nelson were prominent local businessmen, as close as anyone to being
'worthies'. Greenwood outpolled them both easily, taking 46 per cent
of the vote. Class identity in this case displaced social deference. Moreover, by the time that Amos Nelson was economically strong enough
to have attempted to emulate the Williamson model, he had conspicuously moved his residence from Nelson to the Craven district of
Yorkshire, where he began the process of becoming a country squire
whose social field extended well beyond the town in which his mills
were located. If Amos Nelson could not become the embodiment of
the town, few others were in a position to be so. None of the men
whose praises were sung on Charter Day gave his name to folk memory
as legends of the town. Though several people enjoyed high public
esteem for their contribution in a number of walks of life, it was not
until the 1930s that Nelson could be said to have acquired a true local
champion – the black cricketer Learie Constantine, the first man from
a non-political background to be made an honorary Freeman of the
Borough, in 1963.

4

Liberalism to Labour, 1890–1918

Nelson is essentially a political town and political discussions are as regular as the sunset.[1]

The thirty years before the First World War were a period of important change in British politics. There has been no shortage of debate among historians on how this change should be defined and interpreted. Many have seen the period as one in which the main cleavages of twentieth-century political life were formed, with social class becoming the overriding determinant of political identity and allegiance.[2] Much attention in this process has focused upon the emergence of the Labour Party. Some historians have portrayed its rise in the years before the war as an almost inevitable consequence of social and economic changes which wrought the demise of the Liberal Party as the main expression of the working-class vote.[3] Others, however, have sought to demonstrate the continuing vitality of the Liberals. P. F. Clarke, in particular, drawing upon evidence from Lancashire, has suggested the emergence of a new form of Liberalism – 'New Liberalism' – which was much more in tune with twentieth-century conditions and ideas than the old-style Gladstonian variety.[4] In the welter of historical point and counterpoint, it is often difficult to perceive a general pattern; in the diversity of British politics at this time, perhaps there was no single dominant trend.[5] If the example of Nelson were a national paradigm, however, the pattern would be clear. Nelson unequivocally supports the view of the inevitable rise of Labour.

Between 1885 and 1918 Nelson's parliamentary politics were conducted in the constituency of Clitheroe. This county division had been created in 1885, in the redistribution of seats that followed the 1884 Reform Act, which had extended the vote to workers in the county areas. The Clitheroe division was one of a very few Lancashire constituencies never to return a Conservative to Westminster. A radical, progressive political culture was deeply embedded within it, especially in the main industrial townships – Nelson, Colne, Padiham, Brierfield and Barrowford. Conservative (or 'Unionist', as the party was often referred to at this time) support was confined to the agricultural districts, some parts of the ancient borough of Colne, and the town of Clitheroe itself. Political matters were of primary concern to the industrial

population. In Nelson especially there was a flourishing culture of
political clubs. For immigrant workers like the Snowdens or the
Coombes, it was natural that political life should be centred around
Liberalism. They came from areas with a strong background of Non-
conformity and no traditions of deference to a local Tory squirearchy.
The West Riding moorland community from which the Snowden
family migrated to Nelson in the 1880s embodied a radicalism bred of
hatred for landlords and nurtured in Chartism, the pages of Baines's
Leeds Mercury, and Methodism, with its opposition to 'the Drink'.
Arriving in Nelson before the 1884 Reform Act, such immigrants found
themselves voteless, just as they had been in their former home villages.
Their determination to remedy that situation made Nelson, in Philip
Snowden's word, 'a hot-bed of radicalism'.[6] They were often fiercely
independent in a *laissez-faire* vein, as was illustrated by the formation
of an anti-vaccination society in Nelson in the 1880s, which campaigned
against the state's interference in the private life of individuals on health
matters.[7] Their religious leaders were not averse to bringing politics
into the pulpit and expatiating on topics as diverse as drink, military
expenditure and landlordism: 'May we not trace a very large proportion
of the sorrows of the nation to the fact that the English law allows
almost absolute property in land to be the privilege of a few?', queried
Revd W. C. Kendall at Colne in 1890 in the course of a demand for
the nationalisation of land.[8] The more advanced sections of the Liberal
Party embraced many of these issues; moreover, the party had been
responsible for bringing the vote to these county areas by sponsoring
the Reform Act. Election manifestos such as those of Sir Ughtred
Kay-Shuttleworth, who won Clitheroe for the Liberals in 1885, which
emphasised 'Lords Reform', 'Free Trade in Land' and 'Equal Rights
for All', were in harmony with the thinking of many voters.[9] 'The
Liberal club', claimed the *Burnley Radical*, 'is a nightly rendezvous for
men of intelligent political thought.'[10]

Political allegiance, however, cannot be taken for granted. In a
by-election in 1902, following the elevation of Kay-Shuttleworth to
the very House of Lords that he had been seeking to reform, the
Clitheroe seat became one of the early successes (and the first in
Lancashire) of the newly established Labour Representation Committee
(later to be known as the Labour Party). The new MP was the weavers'
leader, David Shackleton. Shackleton had, until just before his election,
been a prominent local Liberal and nonconformist, as well as being an
official of the Darwen Weavers' Association and vice-president of the
Northern Counties Weavers' Amalgamation. His trade-union creden-
tials were impeccable, which explains his selection as the Labour
candidate for the constituency, but his political his views were little
different from those of his predecessor. In this sense, his election as
MP for Clitheroe did not mark a significant departure from the tradition

of political liberalism. However, this parliamentary event should not be allowed to mask the significance of important developments that had been taking place for a decade or more in the grass-roots politics of the area, especially in Nelson.

The key element in the earlier local strength of Liberalism had lain in its relationship with organised religion. The chapels provided a point of access with the working class and thus gave Liberalism a popular appeal. Towards the end of the century, however, other loyalties were being forged. By the late 1880s organised labour was becoming a force to be reckoned with politically. The membership of the Nelson Weavers' Association had risen to around 3,000 by the close of the 1880s. In 1889 its influence was extended through the setting-up of a Trades Council, in which the Weavers forged links with other workers such as warp-dressers, plumbers, cloggers and tailors.[11] The dominance of the Weavers' Association was understandable given their role in the labour force, and it was underlined by the appointment of their secretary, William Ward, as secretary of the Trades Council in 1890, the year of Nelson's incorporation. The coincidence of the borough's first municipal elections and the burgeoning strength of the Nelson weavers was not lost on Ward, who took the lead in proposing that a trade union or 'labour' party should be among the groups contesting for power. In fact, the Weavers' Association went ahead and sponsored two candidates – including Ward himself – together with a third 'labour' man who was not a member of the association. All were radicals, and there was speculation that they might be adopted by the Liberal Party. In the event, only two – Ward and Tattersall (the non-member) – went to the poll and were opposed by the Liberals. They campaigned on a range of moderate issues of practical relevance to working people: economy in town expenditure, fair labour contracts at trade-union rates, cheaper school books, and the abolition of gas meter rents. Both were successful. Tattersall was returned in Whitefield ward, together with two Liberals including John Wilkinson, chairman of the Incorporation Committee, who commanded a strong personal following. William Ward, standing in Walverden, the largest ward in the borough, was returned alongside two Conservatives – J. H. Edmondson, a member of the former Local Board, and J. P. Sunderland, a local cotton employer. This was an interesting result; whereas Tattersall clearly benefited from Liberal support in Whitefield, it seems that Ward's labour platform did have some influence over the voters in what was not normally a strong area for Liberalism.[12]

The suggestion that there might be a place for labour politics independent of Liberalism was not lost on the influential cotton workers' newspaper, the *Cotton Factory Times* (*CFT*). It had followed events in Nelson closely. For the last few years the *CFT* had been conducting a campaign urging organised labour groups to bring out independent candidates in municipal elections. At Nelson, and particularly in the Walverden result, the *CFT* claimed to perceive 'a determination on the part of the industrial classes to put an end to the present unsatisfactory state of class monopoly'.[13] In many other Lancashire towns, however, trade unions fought shy of becoming involved in politics lest partisanship be introduced into their ranks and thereby weaken their industrial strength. This was especially true of the two big trade-union organisations in Lancashire, the cotton workers and the miners. The leaderships of both were concerned that the divided political loyalties of their members would prove to be a stumbling-block in any attempt to promote trade-union political action. Nelson weavers were less inhibited by this, because there was a large degree of political unanimity within their ranks. The prospect of Liberal–Tory antagonism emerging seemed remote. It had been assumed, incorrectly as events proved, that labour candidates would be assimilated into the prevailing Liberal system and adopt the 'Lib–Lab' posture so often found in mining districts.[14]

The refusal of the Liberals to embrace Ward and Tattersall in 1890 was a significant event which pushed organised labour into adopting an independent position that it might not initially have been seeking. Few in 1890 would have seen this as a decisive breach, though subsequent developments did nothing to heal relations. The implantation of socialism in the next few years complicated the picture. Socialism came to Nelson from the outside, bringing with it new political strategies. In 1891 a branch of the Social-Democratic Federation (SDF) was established in Nelson following a speaking tour in the district by Herbert Burrows, one of the SDF's leading figures. The SDF had been a small and mainly London-based radical organisation which, in the mid- to late-1880s had attempted to extend its operations to Lancashire.[15] Its chief aim was to convert industrial workers to the Marxist brand of socialism with which it was increasingly identified at this time. Historians have generally been quick to characterise the SDF as a rigid and somewhat doctrinaire body unresponsive to the needs and interests of trade unions, though this stereotype is not always borne out by a close examination of local development. Members of the SDF were, for example, among those responsible for the formation of the other main socialist tendency to affect the North of England in the late nineteenth century: the Independent Labour Party. Usually associated with Bradford,[16] the ILP's formation also owed much to the activities of socialists in the Manchester and Salford area in the early 1890s and their dissemination of ILP philosophy into other parts of the region over the next few years. A branch was formed in Nelson in 1892. ILPism represented a moral and ethical form of socialism – sometimes drawn from evangelical religion, sometimes from a secular, humanitarian code – which stood in marked contrast theoretically to the

Marxism of the SDF, though in practice this did not prevent the two bodies from co-operating in a number of places, including Salford, Blackburn and Rochdale. Many ILPers were influenced by Robert Blatchford, editor of the *Clarion* and author of the popular socialist book *Merrie England* (1893). Blatchford's main political mission was 'making socialists' rather than electioneering. In this respect, the ILP had much in common with the SDF and, at the local level, it was often their similarities rather than their differences that emerged. Indeed, the ILP was never a fully unified body: recent research has revealed several philosophical and strategic tensions within it.[17] But one objective that was always to the fore in its agitation alongside (and sometimes in opposition to) Blatchford's socialism was the idea of a 'labour alliance'; in other words, the forming of a partnership between trade unions and socialist bodies which would provide a broad base for an independent party of labour in both local and parliamentary politics.

The history of socialism in Nelson reveals many of these features. The essential issue for both movements, as it was for the Liberal Party, was the extent to which they could win the backing of the Nelson weavers. For this reason, both socialist groups directed their propaganda to issues of concern for industry and trade unions. One such issue was the eight-hour day. This had considerable support within the labour movement nationally in the early 1890s, not only because it was considered socially desirable and likely to lead to a reduction in unemployment, but also because the idea of restricting output by working shorter hours seemed a way of setting 'the overstocked markets right', as the *CFT* put it, and restoring some sanity to world trade, which was beset by uncertainties of boom and slump. However, the leaders of all the main cotton unions, fearful of the effect that such a measure might have on the international competitiveness of the cotton industry, had opposed it at Trades Union Congresses (TUC) in the late 1880s. Matters had come to a head at the TUC in Liverpool in 1890, when Mawdsley and Birtwistle, representing the spinners and the weavers respectively, had resigned their seats on the TUC Parliamentary Committee in protest against the delegates' acceptance of the principle of establishing the eight-hour day by legislation. It was, in the opinion of the cotton leaders, a decision calculated to undermine Lancashire's trading position in relation to eastern producers. 'Go to the Government', said David Holmes of the Weavers' Association in disgust, 'and ask the Government to pass a Factory Act for India somewhere near what ours is at home.'[18]

In the face of this stance from county leaders, the SDF in Nelson and elsewhere took up the cause of the eight-hour day knowing that the general decline in trade would support the argument. In the summer of 1891 the Nelson weavers had been urging for an international campaign on the issue; by the following summer, socialist argument had brought the union round to full endorsement of the measure.[19] Even the *CFT*, normally loyal to the leadership of the amalgamated unions, was now asserting that 'what cotton operatives do in other countries will have to be abandoned from all consideration, and what is requisite in this country will have to take its place'.[20] In August 1892 the United Textile Factory Workers' Association, the body through which the cotton unions campaigned for legislative changes to industry, voted in favour of a legal eight-hour day. This represented a remarkable transformation in attitudes which had come about, in large measure, as a result of the persistence and relevance of socialist campaigning, and it brought the socialist parties a good deal of support in the cotton districts.

It was initially the SDF that sought to take advantage of this in Nelson. Its strategy was to win the weavers' support for a labour parliamentary candidate for Clitheroe. In 1892 the weavers had complained that the sitting MP, Kay-Shuttleworth, had been neglecting his duties in the Commons by being absent fom several important divisions. More fundamentally, the question was raised of whether a landowner could properly represent the interests of working men. The weavers, with SDF prompting, even proposed putting up a labour candidate for Clitheroe, though the scheme was dropped when the support of other trade societies in the constituency proved lukewarm. Its main consequence was a further widening of the gulf between organised labour and the Liberal Party, which refused to co-operate with any labour candidates in the 1892 municipal elections. It was this event which occasioned the formal establishment of the ILP in December of that year. Thereafter, a harmonious electoral liaison between socialists and trade unions resulted in the return of three labour representatives to the new School Board in 1893; one stood as a socialist alongside two Trades Council men who fought on a nonconformist ticket. In the same year two labour candidates – William Ward and Thomas Lord of the Weavers' Association – were elected to the Town Council. For these elections, the labour–socialist alliance had put forward five candidates on a platform which included fair labour contracts, improvements in local bathing and gymnasium facilities, municipal housing, and the municipal control of hospitals and public houses.[21] This was an impressive performance which prompted the Liberal *Nelson Chronicle* to comment, following Ernest Johnson's election to the School Board: 'Comrade Johnson is where he is because the socialist is well organized and therefore instead of wasting their strength in vain and useless rivalry they kept well together, and what is more to the purpose, worked together.'[22]

Socialist influence in the Weavers' Association was undoubtedly marked at this time. An indication of this was provided in October 1894, when the cotton unions conducted a ballot, on a district-by-district basis, on the two issues that socialists had been keenly advocating over the previous couple of years – an eight-hour day and labour representation. Generally the spinning sections of the industry favoured the former rather than the latter; in weaving the preference was the other way round. In north-east Lancashire, however, there was a noticeably local trend (see Table 4.1).

Table 4.1. United Textile Factory Workers' Association: Ballot on the eight-hour day and Labour Representation, October 1894

	Burnley		*Padiham*		*Nelson*		*Colne*	
	For	*Against*	*For*	*Against*	*For*	*Against*	*For*	*Against*
Eight-hour day	4250	3498	1175	958	2328	1051	816	274
Labour representation	4239	3009	1117	777	2227	594	742	147

Source: United Textile Factory Workers' Association, *Report of Ballot on the Eight Hour Day and Labour Representation* (UTFWA, Manchester: 1895).

Nelson and Colne in particular demonstrated conclusive backing for both measures, and there seems little doubt that this situation owed something to the socialist campaigns and the success of local labour politics in Nelson. For the remainder of the 1890s, however, little if any progress was made in this direction. Bitterness began to creep into the relationship between the SDF and ILP in Nelson, as the latter seemed to be growing into an all-purpose labour and socialist party which threatened to remove the need for a separate SDF. In 1894 the Nelson SDF went so far as to attempt to prevent its speakers appearing on ILP platforms, and the national hostility that was souring relations between the two bodies at this time added fuel to this local friction.[23] In the wake of this, a poorly attended members' meeting of the Weavers' Association in January 1896 decided by a substantial majority to withdraw from all electioneering.[24] Without the support of the weavers labour representation became a dead letter.

The decision was not rescinded until 1901, when the manoeuvres that led to Shackleton's election the following year were set in train. What had brought about this change? The answer depends to a large degree on national developments. Prominent among these was the formation in 1900 of the Labour Representation Committee (LRC), a body designed to co-ordinate labour forces for the purpose of electing labour MPs to the House of Commons.[25] The LRC was, in effect, a national manifestation of the 'labour alliance' idea, and it was this very body which first floated the notion of David Shackleton as a labour candidate for Clitheroe. The proposal, however, met with mixed reactions locally.

MR D. J. SHAKLETON LABOUR CANDIDATE. CLITHEROE DIVISION 1906.

4.1 David Shackleton (not Shakleton, as this early publicity photograph from the 1906 general election has it) was the first Labour MP to represent Nelson. He was elected in 1902, when Nelson was part of the Clitheroe constituency. A Labour moderate and a trade-union leader, certainly not a socialist, Shackleton earned high esteem in the Labour Party of the pre-war era. He was narrowly defeated for the position of leader (then called chairman) by Keir Hardie in 1906. In 1910 Shackleton renounced politics in favour of a civil service career and became an official, specialising in labour questions, in the Home Office and, later, the Ministry of Labour. From 1921 to 1925 he was Chief Labour Adviser to the government. He was knighted in 1917. (*Lancashire Library, Nelson Local Studies Collection*)

The Nelson weavers, notwithstanding the decision of 1896, were unequivocal. They had maintained a progressive stance in the late 1890s, supporting measures such as 'the socialisation of the means of production, distribution and exchange' and continuing to press for the adoption of legislation for an eight-hour day. At the same time, a number of industrial issues were vexing the weaving trade in the late 1890s: two in particular – the possibility of government action to raise the age of the half-time exemption, and the perceived inadequacy of the clauses in a new Truck Bill to prevent the exaction of fines from workers – added weight to the argument that weavers needed all the parliamentary help that they could muster. Delegates from the Nelson Weavers' Association to the TUC in 1899 were instructed to vote in favour of the motion which established the LRC, at whose foundation conference in February 1900 the Nelson weavers were also represented. In the following year it was decided to overturn the decision of 1896 and to revive local labour politics. A special subcommittee was appointed to organise municipal election campaigns.[26] Similar activity had been taking place in Colne, where the secretary of the Weavers' Association A. B. Newall had been elected to the Town Council. Thus a solid foundation therefore existed from which to build a campaign that might challenge Liberalism for the Clitheroe seat. Exactly who should contest it, however, was a difficult question which produced considerable local acrimony.

It was on this issue that relations between the ILP and SDF in Nelson finally suffered, in the words of the SDF national journal *Justice*, 'a decided rupture'. Much of the initial negotiation on the part of the LRC had been conducted by Philip Snowden, a member of the ILP. Snowden made contact with the local cotton unions and the socialist groups to discuss a possible candidate, and it became clear that, from the ILP's point of view, Snowden himself was the preferred man. In many ways, especially as a former resident of Nelson, he would have been an ideal candidate, but he was a committed socialist and his candidature would undoubtedly have been opposed by the Liberals. An alternative man, one who could bridge the Liberal–socialist–trade-union currents, might have a chance of being unopposed by the Liberal Party. David Shackleton fitted this requirement perfectly and was selected by the Clitheroe Labour Representation Association in July 1902, a month after it had become known that Sir Ughtred Kay-Shuttleworth was to enter the House of Lords. Snowden conceded the point, writing to Newall: 'I think that Mr. Shackleton, as a trade union official and one so thoroughly acquainted with the staple trade and with the labour conditions of the district, has a far better claim and would make a more useful representative.'[27] The decision, however, did not please the local SDF. Their national body, always sensitive to the trade-union influence within the LRC, which was seen as weak on socialism, had withdrawn from the LRC in 1901. This decision was vigorously opposed by both the Nelson and Burnley SDF branches in the interest of keeping relationships between all the labour forces open.[28] But the SDF in Nelson was adamant that any labour candidate for Clitheroe must be a socialist. Shackleton – 'a Labour candidate pure and simple'[29] – offered too ambiguous a stance ('partly satisfactory and partly unsatisfactory') and the SDF refused to support him. By adopting this position on the eve of what was to be a great labour triumph, the SDF effectively shut itself off from subsequent labour developments in Nelson and the surrounding area.

Conversely, by not demurring at the choice of Shackleton, the ILP's stock rose, especially after the successful outcome of the by-election in August 1902 and the subsequent Labour victories in Clitheroe for Shackleton and his successor, Albert Smith, in the three general elections of 1906 and 1910. A well-organised local labour movement, in which the ILP was an important element, emerged in the Clitheroe division during these years. Parliamentary work was the responsibility of the Clitheroe Labour Representation Committee, formed out of the Textile Trades Federation. In contrast with most other areas, where membership of local labour parties was only possible on an affiliated basis, individuals could join the Clitheroe LRC in their own right, at the same subscription rates as those paid by members of affiliated societies. In this way people who were not members of trade unions or socialist societies could still join the LRC. Its executive was elected from each of the different districts within the parliamentary constit- uency, according to the number of voters, and these districts in turn elected their own committees for electoral work in the wards. By the time of the 1906 general election, Clitheroe constituency already had an efficient and well-balanced Labour Party built along the lines which were to become familiar for constituency parties of the future.[30]

Municipal politics were the special concern of LRCs set up in each of the individual towns. In Nelson the Weavers' Association was the backbone of the party, with six representatives. It felt able to identify itself wholeheartedly with Labour, disseminating full details of Labour Party activities at each quarterly members' meeting. The Liberal inhe- ritance was effectively abandoned both in electoral politics, where Labour now felt confident enough to reject belated Liberal overtures for co-operation, and in ideology, where a distinctive Labour platform was being shaped through the efforts of the ILP and the new Labour newspaper, the *Nelson Workers' Guide*. Labour's programme was essen- tially a moderate one, continuing the theme of municipalisation that had been established many years before and urging prudence in expend- iture. Popular success was achieved by the LRC in 1905 by the reduction of the gas rate.[31] So effective was this that, by 1905, the Labour Party, with 15 councillors in the Town Hall, had a working majority in the Council and, the following year, their first mayor, when William Ric- kard succeeded the Liberal (later Conservative) employer of labour, Amos Nelson.

Though its control of the Council was not assured, Labour was now a major political force in the town. In fact, there were some indications that the other parties were moving in the direction of regrouping into an anti-Labour coalition. The *Workers' Guide* claimed to perceive a class realignment as early as 1903: 'It would seem that municipal contests are not to be between Liberal and Conservative, but between Labour and anti-Labour, in other words, between the employer of labour and the labourer.'[32] The analysis is a little premature as far as Nelson is concerned, although moves of this kind were clearly evident in Colne, where the Liberals, led by Alderman Sam Catlow, had realised the danger quickly and had successfully allied with the Tories and the Free Church Council to stem any Labour advance.[33] By 1909, however, when Labour lost control of the Town Council in Nelson, municipal politics were beginning to move towards a similar alignment. The charge that was directed against Labour by its opponents was that of 'extravagance'. The *Colne and Nelson Times* bemoaned the increase in rates under Labour, moderated, it was claimed, only by the success of the gas undertaking (a pre-Labour development) and the achievement of the Conservative-dominated Lancashire County Council and the Burnley Board of Guardians in reducing the Council's contribution to the Poor Rate. Labour plans to pay the Mayor a salary, and their proposal to spend over £10,000 on new public baths, were exploited by their opponents, who looked forward to Labour's removal from power and their replacement by 'practical men' who knew how to conduct business affairs. The terms 'anti-Labour' and 'anti-socialist' were used frequently in the press coverage of these municipal elections. In addressing a post-election meeting at the Weavers' Institute, H. Duerden, the defeated Labour candidate in Central ward, claimed that the party had been forced into fighting the elections on a 'capital versus labour' basis by its opponents: 'Conservatives and Liberals had worked shoulder to shoulder', he said. In Walverden ward, a Labour stronghold, it was noted that the chapel and temperance factions had combined with Liberals and Conservatives to oppose Labour.[34]

Important though all these developments were, they do not convey a full picture of Nelson politics in these years. The emphasis on class as the principal determinant of political behaviour obscures a number of other ideological strains that were present in the town. Religious affiliation, for example, which had been an important architect of political loyalty in the nineteenth century, was still evident in the early years of the new century though its influence was in decline. Probably the last great political battle to have religion as the primary focus of interest was that fought over the Education Act of 1902. The minds of all the denominations in Nelson were exercised over this legislation, which simultaneously abolished the board schools and provided a measure of financial assistance to voluntary establishments through the rates. Initiated by a Conservative government, it was to be expected that Liberal and nonconformist Nelson – which had operated for many years without a School Board and which could usually expect a nonconformist majority on the board after its eventual establishment in 1892 – would find the legislation unwelcome. It was seen as a way of baling out the voluntary educational efforts of the Church and Catholics: 'The object aimed at', claimed the Revd J. B. Buglass of the Barrowford Free Church Council, 'was to knock down Board Schools by endowing and giving to Catholics and Voluntary Schools rates in order to teach sectarian religion.' This, together with the loss of direct democracy that had been embodied in the principle of the elective School Board, formed the brunt of the opposition to the new legislation. It was carried, nevertheless, supported by some of the more powerful local interest groups, principally the Wesleyans, whose schools were amply remunerated under the new arrangements and whose numerical strength assured them of representation on the new Education Committee. Opposition continued well after 1902, however, and many leading nonconformists joined the Passive Resistance movement, refusing to pay the new education rate.[35]

Other strains were to be found within the labour movement itself. Class solidarity did not always produce political harmony. One source of growing tension was the philosophy of the new Labour Party. In spite of the influence of the ILP, Labour was essentially a moderate body. Its MP was scarcely in the forefront of progressivism. Along with most Labour MPs at this time, he showed little interest in, or knowledge of, issues outside the narrow range of trade-union concerns. Foreign affairs, for instance, were given little attention, and even on the 'half-time' question Labour and Shackleton opted for the status quo. There was conspicuous support for Shackleton among sections of Radical opinion, a fact which must have made some ILPers think twice about putting their weight behind him in 1902.[36] There were early indications here of a gulf between ILP and Labour. In other northern constituencies, notably those around Manchester, marked divisions over philosophy and policy were developing, reaching a pre-war peak around 1911, when the Socialist Unity conference in Salford saw ILP branches in the North turn their back on Labour and throw in their lot with the SDF in the newly formed British Socialist Party. This tension was less noticeable in Nelson, though a gulf was certainly to open up after 1914 as a result of the stance taken by Shackleton's successor, Albert Smith, over the war.

Equally significant ideologically was the issue of gender. Of course, women were actively involved in the Labour Party and the ILP, but the extent to which such organisations were able to move away from a patriarchal vision of society is debatable. In an interesting essay on the SDF in Lancashire, for example, Karen Hunt has shown that women were generally marginalised in this party, which tended to see them as something of a 'problem'.[37] Further evidence on this theme is provided by Jill Liddington's wonderfully detailed study of Selina Cooper, which places the discussion in the context of the labour movement in Nelson itself. What is so important about Liddington's analysis is its highlighting of the fact that none of the mainstream political and industrial organisations in Nelson and the surrounding district in the late nineteenth century – ILP, SDF, Weavers' Associations, Liberal Party, even Women's Co-operative Guild – gave much attention or sympathy to the question of votes for women. Notwithstanding the greater degree of gender equality in Nelson, which produced women's participation in trade-unionism and political life, there appears to have been an inability to make the intellectual connection between workplace equality and the idea of votes for women. The conventional response from the labour and socialist movement on this was that gender equality would result from the removal of class inequalities, though women like Selina Cooper and her friend and fellow suffrage activist Harriette Beanland were beginning to argue in the 1890s that the inferior political and legal position of women was an effect of male, rather than class, power. This point was made to great effect by Selina Cooper and the North of England Society for Women's Suffrage at the time of the Clitheroe by-election, when they publicised the position of women trade-unionists (over half the membership of the Nelson Weavers' Association), whose union subscriptions formed a crucial contribution to Shackleton's election expenses, though the women themselves were debarred from voting.[38] In fact, the Clitheroe campaign triggered a powerful parallel campaign for women's suffrage both in Nelson and throughout the North. It saw the establishment of a Nelson Suffrage Committee in the summer of 1906 and the winning of support by Nelson weavers for the adoption of women's suffrage as a trade-union issue. For all that an impressively co-ordinated campaign was set in motion at local and national levels, however, the women's suffrage principle received scant acknowledgement from the powers that be. Selina Cooper was particularly disappointed to witness its rejection by the Labour Party at the Belfast conference of 1907, at which she herself was a delegate.[39]

The failure to carry this measure by no means diminished the role of women in the political life of Nelson. In fact, the importance of women's movements increased, broadening into a number of areas which were to have a profound effect upon the future development of political ideas in the town. Many of these strands became evident during the First World War.

The war brought deep divisions to Nelson, both within the labour movement and in the town generally, threatening to fracture the spirit of community that had developed over the previous few decades. At the outset, there had been a guarded scepticism about the conflict with Germany on the part of many sections of opinion. Church leaders had protested at the declaration of war and, in reporting a jingoistic send-off of ambulance men from Brierfield by a youthful crowd of well-wishers, the *Nelson Leader* had commented: 'the martial spirit is easily fired and the consequences, apparently, lightly considered'.[40] Within a couple of months, however, the *Leader* was adopting a more patriotic stance which was shared by many townspeople, including some sections of the Labour Party. Albert Smith, for example, the former secretary of the Nelson Overlookers who had become Labour MP for Clitheroe in 1910, when David Shackleton took a job with the Home Office, was a keen supporter of the government's policy. He appeared prominently on the all-party recruiting platforms which the three main political organisations had agreed to form, voicing the surge of patriotic enthusiasm that engulfed many places at this time. In Nelson it was responsible for the clamour to enlist when a recruiting station was opened on 12 August 1914. It was estimated by the *Leader* that over 1,000 had been recruited in Nelson by the end of September.[41] Smith himself volunteered at this time and joined the Army as a lieutenant. He was later promoted to captain, by which title he was known forever after. In a speech he made in December 1914 at a farewell gathering to mark his impending departure, organised for him by his own Overlookers' Association, Smith urged his example upon all: 'if all able-bodied men would join His Majesty's forces it would bring the war to a more speedy termination'.[42]

By contrast, the ILP, whose membership in the town at the outbreak of war was somewhere in the region of 1,000,[43] stayed true to its tradition of internationalism and maintained the spirit of anti-militarism which it had been nurturing in previous the months. Andrew Smith, the ILP secretary, had expressed solidarity with German workers in the early part of 1914. They, he claimed, 'were resolutely opposed to increased militarism in their own country'.[44] Because of this, the ILP came to be seen as 'pro-German'. This epithet was especially applied after a visit in October 1914 from Clifford Allen of the No Conscription Fellowship, who gave a speech which was immediately printed as a pamphlet with the provocative title, *Is Germany Right and Britain Wrong?* This, as may be imagined, occasioned strong opposition from the patriotic factions, and Nelson became one of a group of northern towns (which included Halifax and Bradford) where meetings of the No Conscription Fellowship were the subject of fierce harassment, often by soldiers in uniform.[45]

When it became clear, in spite of Albert Smith's hopes, that no speedy termination would be achieved in France, the opposing factions on the war question settled into a hostile confrontation. Early in 1916, with the introduction of conscription under the Military Service Act and the first assignments of 'attested' men leaving the town under Lord Derby's earlier registration scheme, a local tribunal was set up, according to the provisions of the Act, to hear cases for exemption from service. Among these were some sixty applications for the new category of 'conscientious objection'. As in most other places, these cases were usually dealt with unsympathetically. One of the leading members of the Nelson tribunal was Captain Smith himself, now invalided out of the forces after suffering sunstroke in the Gallipoli campaign.[46] The ILP had become something of an organising centre for conscientious objectors, whose numbers were said to be greater in Nelson than in any other town.[47] Moreover, deprived of many of its male activists by this time, the anti-war group came to rely increasingly upon its women members. By 1917 their wartime politics had formed around three main issues: conscription and the treatment of conscientious objectors; maternity and infant welfare; and peace. All three were represented in a curiously incoherent way at a demonstration organised by the Women's Peace Committee in August 1917 which proved to be the ugliest political incident in Nelson during the whole war. The demonstration was to be held on the recreation-ground and preceded by a procession from the public baths. Noise, the threat of violence, and general commotion accompanied the event from start to finish. The procession should have been led by a local band but, according to the *Leader*, none could be found to accept the commission. Instead, it was led by a large force of mounted and foot police who managed to protect the women organisers from assault. At the recreation-ground, however, the general jeering, throwing of sods, and the inability of the speakers to make themselves heard caused the police to suggest closing the meeting after only 40 minutes. The speakers, including Selina Cooper, Mrs Ingham (the mother of an imprisoned conscientious objector), Margaret Bondfield and Mrs Louis Fenn, were unable to put their planned resolution, which had been framed around the idea of a peace without annexations, to a vote. Instead, a rival platform was extemporised by a pro-war group led by Sergeant Major (later Alderman) Bannister and soldiers wearing discharge badges. They articulated a popular belief of the time – that if Germany were not destroyed, the war would have to be fought all over again in 15 years' time by their children. Selina Cooper had intended to use the event to publicise maternity and infant welfare reforms which she had been promoting in Nelson since before the war; the war emergency provided a timely opportunity to advance this issue. The idea of motherhood was now being taken seriously by public authorities sensitive to the issue of population and birth rates: 'Motherhood is the most important feature of the nation's life', proclaimed Nelson's deputy medical officer of health in opening an Infant Welfare Centre.[48] But in the tumult at the recreation-ground, Selina Cooper's message on infant welfare was drowned. The pro-war crowd went off to throw sods at the ILP club in Vernon Street; the advocates of municipal social reform waited a little longer to work their influence in Nelson.

Not only was there an obvious pro- and anti-war cleavage in the town, but conditions undoubtedly sharpened those ideological tensions within Nelson's labour movement which had been developing since the early years of the century – and also brought some new ones. By 1918 it was clear that the ILP was determined to remove Albert Smith from his seat in the House of Commons; over the next four years the party pursued a lively campaign to secure a stronger socialist presence at Westminster for the new constituency of Nelson and Colne. They very nearly ousted Smith in 1918 with a rival candidate for the Labour nomination in the person of R. J. Davies, an ILP man from Manchester. An unsuccessful attempt was made in 1920, when Albert Smith retired, to replace him with Philip Snowden, though the nomination eventually went to Robinson Graham, an official in the Burnley Weavers' Association. The selection of Arthur Greenwood for the general election of 1922, and his victory over strong local Liberal and Conservative opponents, came as partial vindication of ILP tactics over the previous four years. But none of this in-fighting could be said to have undermined Labour's overall strength in the constituency. The pre-war transition to Labour was confirmed in the general election of 1918, which took place immediately the war ended. Albert Smith contested the new seat for Labour in the face of opposition from both within his own movement[49] and from the Liberal Party; he nonetheless achieved a bigger majority (5,452) than had been expected in a poll that was reduced by the failure of many ballot papers to reach men in the armed forces. The *Nelson Leader* accounted for Smith's success by his war record, feeling that his activities had commended themselves to voters with no particular party leanings, who thus gave 'a measure of support which could not have been given to a pacifist'.[50] In local politics, too, Labour's position was much the same as it had been when the war started. The anticipated breakthrough did not come in 1919. Labour was clearly a force to be reckoned with in Nelson, though, as Andrew Smith claimed, sympathy for the party still needed to be turned into votes.[51] Strains had certainly been placed upon the sense of community in Nelson during the years of war, but these had not impeded the main political development in the town; the result in the general election of 1918 neatly encapsulated the changes that had taken place over the previous quarter of a century.

5

Economy under Pressure, 1914–1945

The end of the War will start a race for world supremacy in commerce ... now is the time when manufacturers, and those who are
intending to challenge the Hun for the lion's share of the world's
trade, should be thoughtfully making their plans for the future.[1]

The conventional image of the 1920s and 1930s as a period of unrelieved
business depression and mass unemployment has recently been chal-
lenged. Some historians, chief among them Stevenson and Cook,[2] have
turned their attention away from the areas dominated by the industrial
staples of coal, cotton and shipbuilding and pointed to significant sectors
of growth and prosperity in the British economy at this time. Much of
this prosperity was connected with the development of a consumer
market in and around London. By the 1930s it had given rise to a
quasi-American urban culture of light engineering, shopping and commercialised leisure. It was, according to the writer J. B. Priestley in 1934:

> ... the England of arterial and by-pass roads, of filling stations and
> factories that look like exhibition buildings, of giant cinemas and
> dance-halls and cafes, bungalows with tiny garages, cocktail bars,
> Woolworths, motor-coaches, wireless, hiking, factory girls looking
> like actresses, greyhound racing and dirt tracks, swimming pools, and
> everything given away for cigarette coupons.[3]

However, little of this was evident in the North of England. Nelson
had its Woolworths, to be sure, opened in 1930, and some of the other
features of modern life described by Priestley were beginning to make
their appearance around this time. But, generally speaking, the image
of 'the slump' remains a valid one for much of the North. It is certainly
the case for much of 'cotton' Lancashire, particularly towns like Oldham
and Blackburn, where the production of coarse cotton yarn and cloth
for the Far Eastern market was a dominant part of the local economy,
which suffered high levels of unemployment.[4] In general the interwar
period represented a radical departure from the pattern of prosperity
experienced before 1914.

There can be little doubt that the war of 1914–18 was the turning-point in the industry's fortunes. Rarely can an event of such an unexpected nature (the *Nelson Leader*, for example, gave more space in late July 1914 to the local police sports than to events in Serbia) have produced such a profound set of consequences. The war unleashed a train of events which upset the terms of world trade which had been established in the course of the nineteenth century. To begin with, wartime disruptions forced many overseas importers of British manu-factured cotton goods to intensify the build-up of their domestic textile industries and become producers in their own rights. Subsequently, they were able to nurture their nascent industries behind protective tariffs which made Lancashire goods expensive. India represented a classic example of this process. A further effect of the war was the emergence of export competitors in so-called 'third' markets such as China, where no significant native textile industry existed as yet. The most obvious, though not the only, example of this was to be found in Japan's role as an exporter to China, where it had already moved ahead of the Americans as a supplier of cotton goods to the markets in north China and Manchuria before 1914. In short, by the 1920s, Lancashire's comparative advantage in the world cotton trade was much diminished; the easy dominance it had once enjoyed – especially in India and the Far East – could no longer be taken for granted.

Acute observers of the cotton trade before the war could no doubt have predicted this as a long-term possibility. The trend, though greatly accelerated by the war, was not *caused* by it. As the history of many cotton industries has shown, newly industrialising areas have certain advantages in the establishment of textile production. An example of this was already evident in America, where the once-dominant New England producers had gradually lost their place to the newer industry of the southern states, equipped with up-to-date technology and a workforce unaffected by the traditions of labour organisation and resistance. For Lancashire producers, many of these changes were telescoped into the short period of the war and its immediate aftermath. The suddenness of the process might explain why both employers and workers were slow to respond in any positive fashion. Indeed, some historians have charged the Lancashire cotton industry with inertia, of having failed to reorganise and introduce new machinery in order to meet the challenge of overseas competitors.[5] Whether this charge is a fair one is another matter, however. It gains credibility with the benefit of hindsight, but whether the Lancashire producers could have intro-duced the suggested innovations at the time is less clear. The industry, and weaving in particular, had a history of small-scale production, much of it undercapitalised. The specialisation of production had brought about an extremely localised industry which made re-organisation difficult. This also militated against the introduction of new machinery – since ring spindles produced yarn which worked better on automatic looms, it would require co-ordination across the whole industry to place production on a new technological footing. Moreover, the Lancashire loom was an adaptable machine, especially suited to weaving finer counts, so it could be used by firms who wanted to switch their production from coarse goods when the bottom had dropped out of that market by the 1930s. In all, it is by no means certain that Lancashire's problems in the interwar years were caused by the inertia of management. Indeed, one historian, Sandberg, has sought to rescue employers from the charge of incompetence by demonstrating that they behaved perfectly rationally on most occasions.[6] The situation in which the industry found itself was a complex one, to a large extent historically determined. It is difficult to escape the conclusion that a major reorganisation of the industry at this time would have required a state-led initiative, involving injections of capital and planning skills quite out of keeping with the prevailing governmental philosophies of the period.

Contemporaries were not, however, unaware of the magnitude of the situation that they faced. The *Nelson Leader* in 1930 was clear that what was being experienced was not merely another temporary slump: 'We are passing through an epoch in our industrial life, not one of those periods of bad trade that we have been accustomed to in past years. We see no genuine reason for optimism ...'[7] In truth, Nelson escaped relatively lightly. Though not without its share of problems, Nelson's fine-quality weaving enabled its mills to sell in markets – such as London and the Home Counties – where they not only had a competitive edge, but where consumers were less affected than Indian and Chinese peasants by shifts in world agricultural prices and, therefore, in their purchasing power.

Nevertheless, Nelson's economy was beset by a series of difficulties which became more apparent from the late 1920s. The foremost problem was the failure of the principal sector of the local economy to continue to provide the levels of employment that had come to be expected. Periodic unemployment had been encountered in the past – the situation at the outbreak of war in 1914 was a recent example[8] – but it became a more persistent feature in the interwar years. After the short-term boom of the immediate postwar period, there was never the certainty of regular work. Even at the end of 1922, when unemployment had moderated after the bad year of 1921 and the local press was predicting good prospects for the following year, many were still out of work or on half-time.[9] What is notable about Nelson, though, is that the chances of getting work remained better here than they did in most, if not all, of the other weaving towns. This was especially so in 1922–29, but even in the period of greatest difficulty, between the world financial crisis of 1929 and the recovery of 1933, unemployment was, with two exceptions, lower in Nelson. Apart from a peak of 55 per cent unemployment in the late summer/autumn of 1931 and a rather less dramatic upturn to just under 30 per cent in the spring of 1932, Nelson's employment level was always higher than that of the other major weaving centres of Great Harwood, Blackburn and Burnley. Its unemployment rate ranged (with the exceptions noted) from 6 per cent in January 1929, to just over 30 per cent in late summer 1930 to around 10 per cent in early 1932. In the later 1930s, when unemployment hovered at an average of around 25 per cent in weaving towns, the levels in Nelson remained similar to those of the early 1930s, even dropping below the national average on occasions.[10] In actual terms, it meant that, for most of the 1930s, there were always at least 1,500 men and women registered as unemployed in Nelson and, in bad times, in excess of 8,000.[11]

To concentrate solely on *un*employment, however, is misleading. One of the chief difficulties in Nelson was that of *under*employment. This was noted by the Ministry of Labour: 'At Nelson less than half the machinery was reported to be running and many operatives were working less than their usual number of looms,' noted the *Ministry of Labour Gazette* at the end of 1921. Again, in 1927: 'employment was somewhat irregular and there was an increase in the number of workers employed upon two or three looms instead of the customary four'. The following year: 'At Colne and Nelson there was no improvement; many operatives being unemployed or suspended.' Employers, faced with the uncertainty of the markets, were resorting to the tried and tested tactic, developed in pre-war years to counter bad trade, of temporarily closing mills or putting weavers on short time. Surveys conducted by the Amalgamated Weavers' Association in the mid-1930s revealed considerable levels of underemployment in all the main weaving centres, including Nelson and Colne.[12] Unemployment of between 15 and 32 per cent was recorded in the period from late 1935 to mid 1937. Carey Hargreaves, secretary of the NWA, commented in some detail on the situation in a quarterly report of 1935:

> Fully qualified weavers in large numbers are still working a full week with one or two warps out almost continuously. It is no uncommon thing to go into a weaving shed and find every weaver with one or two warps out, some standing for days at a time with only one warp in ... why do weavers continue to work with half or less looms? Because they are afraid that if they leave their work thay will not be allowed to return until all the weavers who have remained at their work are 'full up' and perhaps not even then. Their fears are fully justified by past experience in many mills.[13]

For most of this time the picture in Colne was bleaker than that in Nelson.

A further point to bear in mind concerns the differential impact of this unemployment on the sexes. Research by Denise Martin into textile workers in the Blackburn and Burnley areas concludes that women experienced higher levels of unemployment than men.[14] Furthermore, the reactions to this in official circles were not always sympathetic. The Anomalies Act of 1931, for example, was introduced to scrutinise claims for unemployment benefit. Its effects were discriminatory on the basis of both sex and marital status, with many married women being disqualified from receiving benefit on the grounds that they had paid insufficient contributions since their marriage.

The position of women workers also came under scrutiny in what became one of the major responses by the weaving employers to the economic problems of the time, the so-called 'more looms' issue. In the past the industry had sought to counter bad trade by a series of expedients: short-time working, adjustments to loom speeds and wage cuts were the principal ones. In the main, there had developed a consensual approach to these problems between employers and workers, at least insofar as the latter were represented by their trade unions. From the 1880s the union leaders in the main sections of the industry had adopted a responsible, managerial attitude towards the development of the industry and liked to think of themselves as equal partners with the employers in the enterprise of cotton production. A number of campaigns had been mounted in this spirit before the war, over issues such as the role of 'middlemen' (brokers and merchants) in pushing up the price of cotton; the bimetallist question of the differential values of gold- and silver-based currencies, which affected trading in cotton goods; and the long-running problems of Indian cotton duties, which had the effect of raising the price of Lancashire cloths in the Indian market. On all these issues there emerged a concerted view between employers and trade unions, causing the socialist writer and analyst Beatrice Webb to describe the cotton industry as 'a union of all the producers in one trade against the outside world'. This view was endorsed by the secretary of the AWA, W. H. Wilkinson, in his evidence to the Royal Commission on Labour in 1892.[15] Consensus was also to be seen in the consideration of technological changes before the war. It was illustrated in the negotiations between leaders of the AWA and Ashton Brothers, a firm in Hyde which took the lead in introducing the automatic ('Northrop' or 'Draper') loom in the early years of the century. One advantage of the new technology, according to the manager of Ashton Brothers, was the opportunity that it offered for labour-saving, allowing married women to leave the mill and stay at home. This was an issue that was to reappear in the industrial conflicts of the early 1930s, when Nelson was at the centre of a series of confrontations which not only fractured the old spirit of managerialism and the consensus upon which it had operated, but which also brought strains to the gender relationships in Nelson's cotton trade.[16]

In spite of the precedent of Ashton Brothers, the idea of confronting the industry's interwar problems by means of a wholesale reorganisation of its technological base does not appear to have been canvassed seriously among employers. There was no doubt as to the general gravity of the situation facing the industry. It was spelled out in plain terms by George Green of Padiham, for example, in a talk that he gave to Nelson manufacturers in 1931, shortly after his return from a mission to the Far East:

> He was convinced that if we hoped to retain our present markets we should have to alter our methods of manufacturing altogether and it would have to be done very quickly. The Japanese were very apt at learning and it was quite common for girls with two years experience to run 10 to 15 ordinary looms ... whilst travelling to Japan he had examined a piece of cloth 2′ 6″ wide 30 yards long and weighing 6lb, shipped and sold at 4s 6d [23p], which could not be produced in this country under 9s [45p].[17]

A little earlier than this, however, the secretary of the county-wide Cotton Spinners' and Manufacturers' Association (CSMA), T. Ashurst, had explicitly disavowed any idea of providing the answer through new looms. 'There is not the money in the industry', he had claimed, 'for the installation of automatic looms.'[18] Addressing the Manchester Rotary Club a few years later, Sir Amos Nelson made a similar point and went on to argue that cloth could not be produced more cheaply than it was in the 'typical' northeast Lancashire mill of 500–2,000 looms.[19]

Instead of new investment and modernisation, the strategy adopted was that of 'more looms'; in other words, increasing the number of looms tended by a single weaver from the customary four to six or eight. This policy produced a number of repercussions at both county and local level in Lancashire during the first half of the 1930s. One of its main effects was a decisive split in relations between capital and labour. Dealings between the two had been worsening in any case in the course of the 1920s as a result of employers' attempts to bring about economies in the trade. Nelson, a well-organised district in trade-union terms, where unemployment had not reduced union membership to the same extent as in other towns, was very much to the fore in the industrial battles of this period. Nelson Weavers took a leading part in industrial disputes over 'more looms' – the county lockout (January–February 1931) and strike (August–September 1932) – and had been engaged in a serious confrontation with employers which had produced a lockout in Nelson itself in 1928.

Before examining the issues involved in 'more looms', it would be helpful briefly to consider the 1928 lockout,[20] which had a powerful impact upon the town, mostly in political terms (to be dealt with in the following chapter). Its importance in economic life lies in the illustration that it provides both of employer–worker relationships at the local level and of relationships within weavers' trade-unionism across the county. A number of established patterns that had been subject to tension since the war were decisively fractured by the lockout.

As Alan and Lesley Fowler have shown, the 1928 lockout came as the culmination of a number of problems that had been building up in the weaving trade during the 1920s. Chief among them were the use of poor-quality yarn, the 'steaming' of sheds to facilitate the easier weaving of this yarn (a practice that had a long history in Lancashire, but which had not previously affected Nelson), and the fining of weavers by cloth-lookers for the production of allegedly bad cloth. All these measures stemmed from an attempt to cut costs and were accompanied by a general intensification of work discipline in the weaving sheds. This included the practice of parading unemployed weavers outside mills as a reminder to those in work of the pool of labour available to replace any recalcitrant employees. Altogether it amounted to a conflict which was essentially to do with, in the words of Alan and Lesley Fowler, 'the question of authority at work and control over the labour process' – a theme which was to have a strong influence over the 'more looms' negotiations.[21] The lockout of 1928 was triggered by a dispute at Mather Brothers when a weaver, John Husband, who was the trade-union representative at the firm and also a member of the Nelson Weavers' Committee, refused to accept a cloth-looker's decision that cloth he had woven was of inferior quality. He refused to pay the resultant fine. The management at Mathers, including the cloth-lookers, might well have felt that the principle of their right to manage was at stake on this issue, and Husband was dismissed. Very quickly the dispute escalated into one which lasted the best part of two months and drew in the county-wide organisations of both the employers and the weaving trade unions.

The principal outcome of the stoppage was the isolation of the NWA as an industrial force. Throughout the dispute, Nelson weavers had been on bad terms both with the employers and their own county amalgamation. When the NWA supported the weavers' strike at Mathers for the reinstatement of Husband, they were confronted by a local lockout – first in the weaving of greys, subsequently in the coloured trade – which was backed financially by the CSMA. The employers seemed determined, as the Fowlers put it, 'to break the strength and tradition of the Nelson Weavers'.[22] The AWA, on the other hand, did not support Nelson in any way, largely because of fears that the Nelson stoppage might spread into a county-wide dispute, with all the problems that such an event would bring. Memories of 1911–12 were still vivid.

Relations between the AWA and NWA were extremely strained, to the extent that Andrew Naesmith, secretary of the AWA, accused Nelson of having 'deliberately engineered a strike' and of treating the amalgamation with 'contempt, derision and indifference'.²³ Added to the county leadership's concern over where Nelson's militancy might push the AWA was also a distaste for the left-wing politics of the Nelson district, where 'communists' had allegedly descended on the town and were manipulating the Weavers' Association.²⁴ Without the backing of the AWA, Nelson's position quickly became untenable and the local weavers were obliged to capitulate to external pressure in the form of a joint initiative from the CSMA and the AWA. A compromise solution offered alternative employment for Husband and a joint investigation into the practice of fining weavers. The weavers at Mathers themselves voted by 99 to 38 to accept these recommendations.²⁵

Though the essential issues of this episode were perhaps of marginal importance compared to the fundamental problems facing the industry, the lockout was nevertheless of great significance in Nelson. It revealed the extent to which capital–labour relations had deteriorated in the town by the late 1920s, and provided the worst possible basis for dealing with the question of foreign competition and the changes that were needed in the industry to face that challenge.

As we have seen, the strategy that the Lancashire employers proposed on this was that of 'more looms'. The idea of re-equipping with new technology was rejected in favour of a system which sought a reduction of labour costs. Six-loom weaving had not been unknown in Lancashire before the First World War, although, according to Wood, it was 'not very prevalent' except in the Burnley district.²⁶ Not surprisingly, Burnley was the area chosen for a pilot scheme of eight looms to a weaver in 1929–30. James Nelson also conducted an experiment with eight looms in Nelson in 1930, paying a wage of 56s. (£2.80) as a fall-back, with a bonus if 80 per cent efficiency was attained. Later in the year Nelsons also tried out a system at Valley Mills (Sheds 1 and 2) which gave the weavers earnings in excess of 60s. (£3.00) a week. The idea of a fall-back wage was important for weavers, because they feared that the new loom ratios would mean a reduction on the old piece-prices and become merely a device for driving wages down. In this case, therefore, Nelsons were being co-operative in fashioning a wage agreement for the eight-loom system which had inbuilt guarantees for workers. The system was, however, gender-biased. Though it involved the application of devices to make the looms semi-automatic and, therefore, secured the backing of the NWA for being technologically innovative, it was nevertheless intended to reduce labour costs and inevitably had the effect of reducing the numbers of weavers needed. The solution proposed, and supported by the NWA, was that the jobs of 'heads of families' (i.e. married men) would be preserved at the expense of those of married women and single people, who would take up the 'ancillary' functions created by the new system.[27] In fact, Nelsons and the NWA came to an agreement on this method of working in the summer of 1931, justified by the old idea of the 'family wage': in other words, a married man would be able to earn enough to keep himself and his family without the need for his wife and dependants to be wage-earners. In practice, though, this illiberal scheme failed to work, simply because the married men by themselves lacked the skills necessary to fulfil the tasks.

Employers generally were not keen to follow the Nelsons lead. They objected to the investment needed to render looms semi-automatic and particularly to the idea of a fall-back payment. Moreover, since Nelsons' system was in part designed to meet new production practices involving artificial-silk weaving – a product likely to command good prices in the market – it was felt that Nelsons could afford the luxury of a fall-back payment where others could not. Wages were at the core of the 'more looms' issue. Employers expected that the new system would increase worker productivity while at the same time reducing wages: wages earned on eight looms would not be double those on four and, effectively, the old list system of wage payment would be abrogated. New lists would be created at mills working on the 'more looms' principle. Much of the acrimony in the trade at this time was to do with loom ratios and wages. The county lockout of early 1931, for example, resulted from a breakdown of negotiations on just such matters. As an increasing number of firms went over to a 'more looms' system, those who remained on the traditional four-loom method and were paid at the old list prices felt at risk, their prices being undercut by the new system. It took over four years of difficult dealing between employers and the AWA before an agreement of sorts was concluded in July 1935 on wage differentials between traditional four-loom weavers and those working on 'more looms', which had now been settled at six. In spite of all this the new arrangement barely scratched the surface of the basic problem of Lancashire's uncompetitive international position.

The Nelson Weavers' Association had always opposed the idea of 'more looms'. Not surprisingly, at a time of high unemployment, they felt the policy was calculated to increase the numbers of jobless and underemployed even further. Nelson weavers it was who notoriously sponsored the famous 'Rebel Delegation' of February 1931 to lobby Cabinet members and MPs against the AWA's policy of negotiating on 'more looms'. They favoured the introduction of new technology, including the labour-saving adaptations to the old Lancashire loom introduced by Nelsons, and more investment to modernise the industry. This, of course, put them at variance with the employers, whose chief concern was to save money rather than spend it. Coming after the animosities engendered by the 1928 dispute, it meant that an atmos-

phere of distrust between capital and labour clouded the discussion
over the future of the industry. For much of the time, employers were
as concerned to maintain industrial discipline and their own right to
determine the strategy to be adopted as they were to arrive at the most
appropriate solutions to the problems of the day. This attitude was
evident in both a general and a particular sense. The Nelson and District
Manufacturers' Association, for example, meeting frequently in 1931
and 1932 to consider the 'more looms' policy, was concerned to ensure
that its own ranks were as solid as possible in the confrontation with
the trade unions. The Manufacturers' Association spent a good deal of
time bringing into line those firms which had broken ranks by running
their looms during the lockout. They also sought to avoid discussion
of whether the 'more looms' strategy was appropriate, some representatives clearly fearing the industrial consequences if it were to be
applied in a town like Nelson. A determination to seize and keep the
initiative on the policy was particularly evident in the manner of the association's chairman, Joe Nelson, son of Amos and a director of the
family company, who reminded members on several occasions that the
real issue at stake was whether employers were to be allowed to manage
their own places of work.

> If we attempted to introduce any system to try to cheapen production
> which differed from the old methods of working we were met by
> resistance from the Operatives. We could choose to accept that
> resistance and let the trade gradually die away, or insist on trying
> new methods with the object of recovering some of our lost
> trade.[28]

His father was expressing a similar viewpoint at the same time: 'the
trying to prohibit more looms ...', he told a meeting of cotton employers in May 1931, '[is] overstepping anything which the trades unions
were expected to do'.[29] Sir Amos also campaigned for the removal of
the uniform list. Nelson was one of only a few places where the list
was largely adhered to by employers in the early 1930s. There was a
drift away from it in other districts, with firms using the 'more looms'
principle as a means of setting new rates. In this free-for-all, employers
became worried about what they termed 'unfair competition' – the
undercutting of their prices by manufacturers using cheaper labour
elsewhere. H. H. Sunderland summed up the Nelson manufacturers'
anxieties in July 1932: 'It would ... only be a question of time before
we had to weave out and the trade would go to the other parts of the
County where the [lower] wages were paid.'[30]

    In the summer of 1931, at the instigation of the Town Council, the
Manufacturers' Association in Nelson reluctantly agreed to meet to
consider a scheme proposed by the mayor to put warp-stop and weft-

feeler motions on the looms, technical adaptations to increase the efficiency of the machinery. The mayor felt that the NWA would be prepared to consider this as a solution. But the employers only agreed to meet the weavers for an informal discussion if they were given an assurance that their attitude on more looms without weft-replenishing motions would be 'other than a blank refusal to negotiate'.[31] Shortly afterwards, the employers restated their basic position: 'whether or not the Operatives liked the system, there was no hope for the trade unless this or some other method of *reducing costs* [author's italics] could be agreed'.[32] Even so, a liaison between the two sides was not out of the question, but its establishment was delayed by a more particular manifestation of employer intransigence: the decision in 1931 by Haightons, of Park Shed, Barrowford, unilaterally to adopt the eight-loom system and to sack any workers who objected.

The Haighton affair rocked Nelson to its core in the summer of 1931. Haightons had introduced an eight-loom shift the previous year, extending it to a double shift in the spring of 1931. This became the subject of a series of demonstrations organised by the NWA against the firm and its imported blackleg labour which culminated in serious clashes between NWA members, bystanders and police in Pendle Street outside the Weavers' Institute, on 11 May. It was followed a few days later by a protest meeting of some 20,000 people on the recreation-ground, at which the action of the police on the previous occasion was emphatically condemned.[33] In spite of all this, Haightons continued with their 'more looms' policy (the only firm in the area actually to put it into practice at this stage), only withdrawing it during the strike in the summer of 1932, when, like all other firms in the district, they shut down.

It is easy to understand why Nelson acquired a reputation for militancy during the late 1920s and early 1930s. The fusion of industrial and political conflicts in these years seemed to keep the town at a high pitch of activity, keeping alive the idea of 'Red Nelson' that had emerged during the 1928 lockout. It must be borne in mind, of course, that a considerable level of industrial militancy was reached throughout cotton Lancashire during these years. The 1932 'more looms' strike was in fact the last of the large-scale strikes in British industry until those of the later 1950s in shipbuilding and engineering. Nelson was not alone, therefore, in having a disturbed period of industrial relations. But the town was exceptional in its behaviour, usually taking an independent course of action in relation to both employers and trade-union federations. This was typified in the rebel delegation, which county union leaders tried to defuse by saying that it was not representative of general opinion. Employers certainly regarded Nelson as a place apart, quick to explain its militancy in terms of 'communists' or 'socialists'. Amos Nelson, not a man usually given to hysterical outbursts, blamed both for having

5.1 A Nelson weavers' demonstration in 1936 for a minimum wage. In an endeavour to meet foreign competition, technical changes and an increase in the number of looms to be supervised by individual weavers had put an end to the old district wage lists and had driven wages down. The importance of women workers, both economically and politically, is underlined by this photograph, which also shows the striking figure of Bessie Dickinson (to the right, wearing a tie), a local Communist Party campaigner for weavers' causes. (*Documentary Photography Archive, Manchester*)

gained control of the trade unions and created an intransigent attitude among the workers, leading them to believe for the past twenty years that they could get more pay for less work.[34] Undoubtedly, communists and communist organisations were involved in Nelson's trade-unionism, but their influence was usually exaggerated by observers – especially the Liberal press. Nelson had a long tradition of ILP politics and it was here that the beliefs of many weavers' officials had been nurtured. But the ILP was essentially political in its outlook. It was not an organisation which sought to foment industrial trouble for political ends, and it is doubtful whether the industrial disputes of this era can be ascribed to specifically political causes. It is much more likely that an explanation for Nelson's militancy is to be found in the strength of trade-union coverage of the workforce, the willingness of men and women to combine together and support each other, and the way in which the nature of their local product enabled the town to escape the worst effects of the slump. It was this that kept the possibility of work open and, therefore, guaranteed that trade union membership would be maintained. Nelson weavers were able to fight to prevent conditions deteriorating because their organisation was stronger than those in other towns, where the depression had hit harder. They were the beneficiaries of relative prosperity, even in the bad times of the 1930s.

How far their militancy aided the long-term prospects of the local

economy is a more difficult question to answer. It is at least arguable
that none of the industrial activity of the 1930s, from both sides of
industry, was at all relevant to the problem of Lancashire's economic
position. One school of thought maintains that without the wholesale
introduction of automatic looms, which the employing class ruled out,
Lancashire was not equipped to face the overseas challenge. Others
have argued that Lancashire was doomed in any event, the victim of
historical circumstances which now gave a comparative advantage to
its competitors. Anything that failed to recognise either of these two
situations was merely whistling in the wind. Where Lancashire did still
hold some trump cards, however, was in the production of high-quality
goods, the very cloths that were manufactured in Nelson. Some of the
most important developments in the economy of Nelson during the
1930s therefore took the form of measures to strengthen these advantages. They had to do largely with the growth of James Nelson's business.

It was during the interwar years that Nelsons developed from a local
into a national and, in some respects, international firm. Shortly after
the death of James Nelson himself in 1912, the company had been
converted to limited liability status. After the war, when the demand
for its high-quality poplins had been great, both from HM Forces and
from its overseas buyers, Nelsons began to branch out. A range of
companies was bought to carry out particular functions under names
other than Nelsons. A. T. Dyer and Co., for example, became the
marketing branch of the firm, while C. Wilkinson and Co. serviced the
overseas demand for poplins, with stock depots in a number of European
capitals. In addition to the increased scale of operations, there was a
radical new initiative in the type of product. The long-established
Bradford textile firm of William Rogerson was acquired in 1930 to
produce rayon fabrics, and it was in the development of artificial fibre
that Nelsons made their most significant contribution to economic
development on a local, and possibly even national, scale at this time.

Rayon, an artificial product derived from cotton linters and wood
pulp, had been developed by the old silk-producing firm of Courtaulds
before the First World War. But it was not until after the War that,
as a consequence both of technical improvements in its manufacture
and changes in fashion styles, the price of rayon dropped steeply and
it became a viable product to compete with wool and silk (though not,
at this time, with cotton). Britain lost some of its early ground in rayon
production to the USA, Germany, Italy and Japan, but it still produced
about 10 per cent of world output by the late 1930s, with Courtaulds
and British Celanese being the dominant manufacturers.[35] Nelsons came
into the business at an early stage, with research being undertaken in
the early 1920s into acetate and viscose spinning for the production of
rayon yarn. Nelsons Silk Ltd was established at Lancaster in 1927 to
produce acetate yarn, and this plant continued in production until it

was closed in the wartime concentration scheme in 1941. Another company – Lustrafil Ltd – was registered in 1923 to develop viscose yarn. (Nelsons hoped that the brand name 'Lustrafil' would become the common term for what was known at the time as 'artificial silk'; customers, it was thought, would be deterred by an 'artificial' substance. 'Rayon' was the term adopted instead.) Valley Mills produced viscose yarn from 1924 and work was conducted on improving the machinery, which produced better-quality yarns by the early 1930s. By this time, under the direction of Joe Nelson, experiments were under way with the continuous filament spinning process rather than the spool-spun method. Prototype machinery was ready in 1935 and the first continuous spinning of Lustrafil was achieved in 1939. Amos Nelson had long since conceived the idea of establishing production plants for the new processes in overseas markets. In the late 1920s he had visited Australasia to view possible sites for rayon production in both Australia and New Zealand and to investigate the possibility of emigration for Lancashire workers. By the time of his death in 1947 he was on the point of opening a plant in Tasmania and well over three-quarters of all Nelsons' output was rayon cloth.[36]

These were important business developments in a town whose economy did not otherwise see much diversification in the interwar period. Whereas Burnley acquired some new light engineering industry in the 1930s, Nelson changed little in essentials. A number of firms closed because of the poor trade of the decade, so that by 1939 there were only half the number of cotton firms operating in Nelson that there had been in 1914, and only 56 per cent of the number in existence in 1928.[37] This trend was continued during the Second World War, as the cotton industry was 'concentrated' to direct labour and raw materials to essential munitions industries. A Ministry of Supply order of 1941 meant that a licence was required to operate looms, and this resulted in the creation of a smaller nucleus of mills under the general supervision of a 'cotton controller' based in Manchester. Altogether, by mid-1945 the weaving industry had lost approximately half of the labour force that it had commanded in 1937, with a consequent halving of its output of all types of cloth over the same period.[38] In Nelson this had had the effect of reducing the number of cotton manufacturers to about 60 by 1942. It continued to produce its poplins for Forces' uniforms, together with surgical dressings, rubber-proofed fabrics and nylon parachute material, of which Nelsons were weaving up to 300,000 yards a week by 1944.

One effect of the Cotton Control Board scheme in Lancashire was the redirection of labour away from cotton. Districts in the vicinity of munitions factories experienced this to a considerable degree, and it caused problems of labour shortage in textiles after the war, when the cotton industry was seeking to re-establish itself in a position of full employment in the economy as a whole. Nelson was less affected by this trend than many other places, largely because of the relative absence of alternative employment nearby. The town's isolation again proved a factor in its development. Some expansion was seen during the war years in Nelson's engineering sector. In 1945 there were some 20 firms operating in metal or electrical engineering, including British Thomson Houston, which had set up at Marsden Mill. But Nelson was still a cotton-weaving town at the end of the war, and had still not found an answer to the question of Lancashire cotton's place in the international economy. The 'plans for the future', recommended so readily at the end of the First World War, had hardly been formulated, let alone implemented, by the end of the second.

6

Red Nelson? Interwar Politics

Do you come from that place up North called Little Moscow? [1]

The term 'Little Moscow' crept into the political vocabulary of Nelson during the lockout of 1928, when the *Nelson Leader* ran the headline 'Moscow Calling'. There was, to be sure, some Communist Party influence in the town at this time, though it could scarcely be described as a dominant presence and, as the *Leader* recognised, it exerted little effect inside the NWA. To call Nelson a 'Little Moscow', suggesting a left-wing political culture deriving its inspiration from the Bolshevik Revolution of 1917 and the Communist Party of Great Britain (CPGB), formed in 1920, is somewhat misleading. However, the idea of Nelson as a centre of 'red' politics – that is to say of progressive, socialist ideas and policies rather than of specifically communist influence – is a valid one and has origins that stretch back farther than the events of either 1928 or the revolutionary ferment that affected Britain just after the First World War.

To some extent the origins can be traced to Nelson's pre-Labour past. As we saw in Chapter 4, the combination of trade-union and socialist interests had produced a strong labour movement in Nelson by the early years of the century. Even during the phase of Liberal politics on the Local Board and in the early Borough Council years, however, a marked emphasis had developed on municipal initiative in politics. The local state, so to speak, was given an important role in political affairs before the arrival of labour as a force to be reckoned with. In this sense, the Labour Party took over this tradition, grafting on to it its own political ideas. For example, public utilities such as gas, water and transport had been vested in municipal control from an early stage. The Charter Day procession of 1890 had in many ways been a celebration of this public initiative. The Labour Party added its own contributions to the body of services provided municipally during its spell in power between 1905 and 1909, though it was always careful to keep in mind the effects of such schemes on the rates and the need for shrewd housekeeping. This sensibility continued to be a part of Labour's strategy when it was returned to power in the later 1920s. The fact that Nelson had both a large working-class population and a high proportion of owner-occupiers meant that Labour had to pay close attention to the level of rates if its vote-winning appeal was to remain strong in a period of economic depression. In some respects, the position of Nelson's Labour Party in the 1920s and 30s, requiring as it did a delicate balance between state provision and public spending, prefigured that of the national Labour Party some 50 years later.[2]

The most distinctive contributions to public services in Nelson between the wars were to be found in the areas of housing, health and welfare. As regards housing, the Liberal-controlled Town Council of the immediate postwar years had been quick to seize upon the opportunities provided by the 1919 Housing and Town Planning Act (the so-called 'Addison' Act). This legislation allowed for the building of houses by local authorities with government assistance. Some 270 houses were constructed in various parts of the town under these provisions, most of the building being in the St Paul's district and in a new estate created in Marsden Park. Additional phases of building under the terms of the 1923 and 1924 Housing Acts (the latter being the most important social measure of the first Labour government) added considerably to the Marsden Park development and also saw the opening of a new estate at Hodge House. Altogether over 500 houses were built following the Acts of 1923 and 1924. Subsequently, following legislation in 1930 (sponsored by the MP for Nelson and Colne, Arthur Greenwood, as Minister of Health) and 1935, Nelson Corporation constructed over 175 houses and bungalows for the aged, a relatively unusual measure for this period. Some of the houses that were built during this period were available for sale but the vast majority were for rent at between 7s. 6d. (36p) and 10s. 3d. (52p) a week. These initiatives crossed party political boundaries. They formed a continuum of urban housing policy during the inter-war period which contributed to Nelson's acknowledged reputation for the quality of its housing stock. 'No area in the district', commented the medical officer of health in his report of 1931, 'can be classed as unhealthy, nor can we regard any group of houses as slums ...'.[3] In a national review of slum property, conducted in the wake of the 1930 Housing Act, Nelson was one of 33 local authorities to be deemed to have no serious slum problem.[4]

Good housing was a contributory cause of good health, in which Nelson displayed a similarly progressive record of achievement. By the early 1930s the Corporation was sponsoring a wide variety of health services, including a daily clinic for schoolchildren and a weekly maternity and child welfare session provided jointly with the county authority. Free milk was available in 'necessitous' cases for expectant mothers and infants, and a maternity home – Fernlea – was opened in 1921 which had space for ten mothers to be attended by their GP and, if necessary, a consultant appointed by the local authority. There was an admission charge for Fernlea, but the Council operated a scheme whereby this could be paid by instalments and was willing to consider applications

6.1 Municipal housing in the Marsden Park area. Even before the Labour Party established its dominance of local politics in the late 1920s, Nelson Borough Council had
taken advantage of postwar Housing Acts to create pleasantly landscaped residential
areas where most dwellings were available for rent. Ringstone Crescent (top), with its
large recreation-ground and views over to Pendle Hill, offers a particularly pleasing
environment. By the early 1930s, over 400 houses had been built in this aea, mostly
under the terms of Wheatley's 1924 Housing Act, passed during the first Labour
government. Altogether, almost 800 had been constructed in the town under the
aegis of the Council by the 1930s.

for free admission. Of the 200 admissions in 1931, 88 paid the full fee of 3 guineas (£3.15) a week, and 100 mothers were granted a reduced fee. Special emphasis was given in other respects to the needs of schoolchildren. Low-cost milk was provided for 1d. (½p) at Bradley Fold Infants' School, and the effects of this were monitored through regular weighing. All schoolchildren who could demonstrate their need qualified for free school dinners (and, in some cases, tea). The establishment of an open-air school in 1930, with an emphasis on games, good nourishment, fresh air and after-dinner rest, was commended by Dr Markham, the MOH, as an innovation linking health and education. In addition to these services provided by the municipality, the townspeople of Nelson could also rely, through county provision, on clinics for the treatment of TB and VD and a voluntary hospital – the Reedyford War Memorial Hospital – to which the Corporation was a major subscriber.[5]

Perhaps the brightest star in the welfare firmament was the maternity and child welfare clinic which had first made an appearance during the war. The idea of having such a clinic originated, in fact, before the war with the campaign of Selina Cooper, Harriette Beanland and members of the Women's Co-operative Guild and the Women's Labour League. This had eventually caused the Council to set up a modest provision in 1917. From these beginnings, Nelson developed a policy on maternity and child welfare which, as the research of Jane Mark-Lawson has shown, consistently provided more financial support in the interwar years than was found in most other towns.[6] Ante-natal care, for example, was well above the national average. Frequent sessions were available, some in the evening to accommodate women who continued to work; it was estimated, in fact, that two-thirds of women worked beyond six months of their pregnancy, some of them right up to the time of their confinement. Municipal midwives were then in attendance for the post-natal care of children up to the age of 5. This provision ensured a good record in one of the chief measures of health care. Throughout the interwar period, Nelson experienced a decline in the rate of infant mortality. In contrast to most towns with a high proportion of working women (Burnley being one), the levels of infant mortality in Nelson were remarkably low. Whilst, as John Walton has observed,[7] the causal relationship between mortality and environmental factors is difficult to pin down, it seems likely that the early provision of good child care in Nelson was a powerful contributory factor in lowering infant death rates. In 1922 Dr Markham reported the lowest rate of infant mortality for many years, together with relatively low levels of sickness and disease. Interestingly, however, he pointed to a differential infant mortality rate within the town: the rate per 1,000 live births in the inner (older) wards of Central (102) and Whitefield (113) was almost double that of the outer (newer) districts of Walverden, Netherfield and South-

field wards (47, 56 and 58). This suggested a very close link between
mortality and social deprivation. In commenting on the report, the
Nelson Leader was in no doubt that the general lowering of mortality
rates was attributable to the policy of the local authority on health:
'We have not much to complain of in Nelson at the way the Council
looks after the health of its people ...'.[8] Some ten years later, Markham
was recording the lowest infant mortality figure ever for the town –
44 per 1,000 births. Attention to the needs of children was always
particularly keen, as is shown by the diligent and comprehensive monitoring of the health of schoolchildren, including those evacuated to
Nelson from cities such as Bradford and Manchester during the Second
World War.[9] This provision, allied to the generally good quality of
housing and even, according to Dr Markham, the nutritional value of
fish and chips (there were some 34 fish and chip shops in Nelson in
the late 1930s), combined to produce a local health service that was
highly praised in a Ministry of Health report of 1937. Nelson might
almost have been a blueprint for the ideas in health and welfare that
came to form the basis of the welfare state in the years after 1945.

Thus Nelson already had a record of progressive municipal reform
by the time that the Labour Party came into its period of extended
municipal power in 1927. The feature of an all-party consensus in social
welfare is underscored if attention is directed to educational provision,
where a reorganisation into an infants–junior and secondary structure,
along the lines advocated nationally in the Hadow Report to the Board
of Education in 1926, had been inaugurated by the local Liberal administration in 1926 under the chairmanship of J. H. S. Aitken and
continued by Labour. The new scheme was completed in time to receive
a 50 per cent grant from the Board of Education before such grants
were axed by the National Economy Act in October 1931.[10] By the
standards of the day, then, Nelson was clearly a town of exceptional
vision in welfare terms. Public – as opposed to voluntary – services
were an accepted feature of the political system. The popularity of this
type of municipal socialism had much to do with the benefits that it
provided for working-class voters, many of whom were working women.
The charge on the rates, the level of which became the major political
issue of the 1930s, was nevertheless accepted in principle because the
public provision was of a high-quality and was unlikely to have been
obtainable any more cheaply on the open market.

In accounting for the variations in the content and practice of social
welfare provision at the local level some historians have stressed the
importance of women.[11] Municipal socialism was attractive to the working class generally, but it was specifically attractive to its female
members. There seems good reason to think that welfare figured
prominently in the politics of Nelson because of the presence of women
not only in the labour force, but in the political domain itself. All

political parties were conscious of the need to cultivate the women's vote, especially after the Reform Act of 1918, which brought women over the age of 30 into the electorate. Contrary to the long-expressed stereotype of the 'conservative' woman, there was a clear recognition in Nelson that women added considerably to progressive thinking: 'they are the stuff that sentimental socialists are made of', declared the *Leader*, creating its own stereotype, but at least acknowledging the idea of a radical female.[12] All parties sought to integrate women into their ranks, but the Labour Party probably succeeded best. There was a long tradition of female involvement in the ILP and related organisations, such as Selina Cooper's Women's Peace Committee. Increasingly, as the life of Mrs Cooper reveals, the Labour Party became the natural home of feminist and women's issues. Its cultural life was well attuned to both sexes,[13] and its Women's Section was an active political force. The mass demonstration that it organised in 1932, for example, against the effect of the means test on women, was a powerful sign of the organisation's presence in the town.[14] It was regarded within the movement as one of the largest such bodies in the country.[15] In a less political sense, also, the Labour Party attempted to make contact with women through a series of domestic links – through socials and 'at homes', to be sure, but also through such events as lectures. One, advertised in the Labour Party newspaper and sponsored by the Corporation's Gas Department, involved representatives of the Radiation cooker company who came to demonstrate the new art of gas cookery.

Considering the place of women in the local economy, together with the traditions of public intervention in the provision of social services, there is good reason to believe that a distinctive brand of municipal socialism would have developed in Nelson whatever the political leanings of its Council might have been. As it was, Nelson became a Labour fief after 1927. Though, with the leaven of Colne, its parliamentary politics were often marginal, Nelson itself became one of those Labour strongholds where commentators jokingly remarked that the votes were weighed rather than counted. This was particularly so after 1934. The return to power of Labour in 1927 had been achieved with only a small majority on the Council, secured by the election of Labour aldermen. By 1934, however, Labour controlled 29 of the 32 places on the Council, and thereafter the opposition was given little encouragement that this state of affairs could be reversed. Labour's dominance of the local political scene undoubtedly added to the town's reputation as a 'red' centre in a number of different ways. Chief among these were a series of incidents associated with the industrial unrest of the late 1920s and early 1930s. They marked Nelson out as an exceptionally vigorous area of agitation, much of it emanating from the Nelson Weavers' Association. The Weavers set their face against 'authority' on several occasions – whether in the form of employers, their own trade-union

leadership, the County Council, or the county-controlled police force.
During the 'more looms' dispute of 1931–2, for example, officials of
the NWA used their influence more than once to prevent their parent
body, the Amalgamated Weavers' Association, from negotiating with
the employers over wages and loom:weaver ratios. This even took the
form of despatching a deputation to London in early 1931 – the
celebrated Rebel Delegation – to lobby ministers and MPs against the
AWA's policy of negotiating with employers. It succeeded in influenc-
ing, among others, Arthur Greenwood, the MP for Nelson and Colne
and the Minister of Health, and was an important tactic in bringing
about the collapse of the 1931 employers' lockout. More dramatic still
were the demonstrations accompanying the adoption of the eight-loom
system at Haighton's mill in Barrowford. These climaxed during May
1931 in clashes between demonstrators and police outside the Weavers'
Institute in Pendle Street and, later in the same week, in a monster
meeting of some 20,000 people on the recreation-ground. The disturb-
ances in Pendle Street, during which a man was arrested and charged
with assaulting police officers, were seen by many as the outcome of
overzealous policing of an industrial dispute – 'Prussian police methods',
as one member of the Town Council described them.[16] In fact, one
bystander (a local headteacher) who was returning from a cricket match
whose crowds had augmented the numbers already present in Pendle
Street, concluded that 'had all the police been as calm, and composed
as the crowd, there would have been no ugly incidents'. Following an
enquiry into the events by the Town Council, the conclusions of which
gave some credence to this view, the matter was pursued by the weavers
with a demand to the Home Office that the police officers involved in
the demonstrations be disciplined. However, J. R. Clynes, the Labour
Home Secretary, declined to take action, feeling that the police had
acted properly to maintain order.[17]

   These episodes revealed a determination on the part of both main
branches of the labour movement not to kowtow to authority. If the
NWA was the protagonist in industrial matters, the Labour Party,
through its representatives on the Town Council, was equally committed to stating its case in other spheres and following it through.
Controversy immediately attended the Labour return to office in 1927.
The replacement of three retiring Liberal aldermen by Labour nominees and the vesting of the mayoralty in the veteran ILPer Andrew Smith
provoked a storm of protest in the Liberal press. It meant that men
like Smith, an anti-war activist of 1914–18, and Richard Bland, who
taught Esperanto (which he had learnt in prison as a conscientious
objector during the war) and who promoted the 'No More War'
movement in Nelson, were now in positions of considerable power.
Influenced by such people, the Labour-controlled Town Council
adopted a distinctive and truculent stance during the industrial disputes

of 1928 and 1931–2. Though not, of course, a party to the disputes itself, the Council made no attempt to stay neutral, still less to take the part of the establishment against the worker. The political position of the Labour councillors was, to a large extent, dependent upon the votes of the men and women involved in industrial action and this explains the benevolent role that the Council adopted towards the trade-unionists on these occasions. The role included the orchestrating, through a subcommittee, of a series of events in conjunction with voluntary associations to promote the 'welfare of the townspeople'. In 1928 the Council reimbursed Salem Chapel for the cost of employing an attendant to keep its infants' school in Scotland Road open as a workers' reading-room during the lockout. Admission charges for the public baths, municipal tennis courts and bowling greens were reduced to half-price, free concerts were staged in municipal parks, and bowling tournaments were arranged. These publicly funded events were, in one sense, an attempt to provide recreation during a period of enforced idleness, but in another sense they represented an official gesture of solidarity with trade-unionists. Moreover, in the person of the mayor, the Council even took on a mediatory role in attempting to bring the two sides of industry together in the hope of reaching a settlement.[18]

A similar position was assumed in relation to external public bodies, often politically Conservative, whose policy stance was crucial for working people at times of economic depression or industrial stoppages. The Burnley Board of Guardians was one such body, responsible for administering poor relief in the Nelson and Burnley area until 1929. During the 1928 lockout the board refused relief to people thrown out of work, except as a loan to be repaid, and refused to receive a ratepayers' deputation from Nelson to discuss this decision. On this occasion, Nelson Council protested formally against the attitude of the guardians[19] and it did the same against the Public Assistance Committee (PAC) of Lancashire County Council, set up by the Local Government Act of 1929 to replace the old guardians. The PAC replicated many of the Conservative attitudes of its predecessors. Frequently, business transacted between the PAC in Preston, with powers to countermand local decisions, and the Labour-dominated Guardians' Committee of District 6 (including Burnley and Nelson) took on a party political character, with local representatives like Andrew Smith, W.J. Throup and Selina Cooper trying to extract as much relief as possible for underemployed workers whom the PAC regarded as being in full-time employment.[20] Following the election of the National Government in 1931, unemployment benefit was to be 'means tested' after 26 weeks and, in assessing 'means', PACs were obliged to take into account all household income. In the late summer of 1932 the Nelson Guardians' Committee, headed by Andrew Smith, took the step of dissolving itself in protest against the PAC refusal to give a liberal interpretation to 'needed' household income. The Town Council, together with the Labour Party and the local trade unions, was active in campaigning against the means test during 1932, especially for the way in which it discriminated against women, three-quarters of whom were estimated to receive no further benefit after the initial six months because of the family income rule.[21]

These campaigns had specific targets, but they were also a reflection of a certain loss of power by local councils and democratic bodies. Nelson Town Council seemed determined that, as an elected body, it should exercise as much responsibility as possible over the welfare of its citizens. This partly explains the succession of issues during the 1930s in which Nelson was in conflict with national authorities. When unemployment was displaced by foreign affairs as the foremost issue in British politics in the late 1930s, the conflict between municipality and state became concerned with matters of militarism and war. Labour women were especially active, with Mrs Cooper again prominent, in maintaining Nelson's old pacifist stance by campaigning for disarmament and peace. In 1934 a procession of some 500 people from a range of political and religious organisations, with banners proclaiming 'Workers Unite against War', 'Peace Our Hope' and 'Mothers of England – Shall Youth Be Slaughtered?', marched to the recreation-ground to hear Councillor Titherington's strong denunciation of war and armaments. In directing this invective against the British government's defence programme, there were clearly deep fears of a repetition of the horrors of 1914–18. Pacifist sentiment had a strong purchase in the town, so these manoeuvres were hardly to be dismissed as the rantings of a lunatic fringe. The British Legion Remembrance Day parade of 1934, for example, was subjected to a counter-demonstration organised by the Nelson and District Anti-War Committee, headed by Regent Street Methodist Boys' Brigade. In the same year, the Nelson League of Nations Union had organised a peace ballot, distributed to over 16,000 households. The responses revealed overwhelming support for the principles behind the League of Nations but, significantly, a large minority of votes was cast against the use of military methods to reinforce the league.[22] There was some popular foundation, therefore, for the positions taken by political leaders in the course of the decade. In 1930, for example, the mayor refused to allow patriotic themes to be worked into celebrations for Empire Week, including a ban on the Iniskilling Fusiliers performing at concerts on the grounds that their presence might jeopardise pacifism by encouraging recruitment to the Army.[23] Later in the decade, when legislation required local authorities to set up civil defence measures against aerial bombardment and empowered chief constables to take action should local authorities decline to do so themselves, Nelson Council responded quickly: it refused to conduct gas drill, dismissed the government's air

6.2 A 'Peace Charabanc' prepares to enter the hospital procession in the early 1920s. Mrs Selina Cooper (to the right of the banner) was a redoubtable campaigner for many progressive causes – including women's rights and disarmament – from the 1890s until her death in 1946, and helped to make Nelson a centre of pacifist sentiment from before the First World War. (*Lancashire Library, Nelson Local Studies Collection*)

raid precautions as 'war propaganda' and allowed the Peace Council to hold its meetings in the Council Chamber.[24] The Council did not go so far as to defy Parliament, but it made its pacifist views very plain. Sydney Silverman, as MP for Nelson and Colne, was one of the Labour MPs who did not support either the Emergency Powers Act or the Conscription Bill in the autumn of 1939, and he was one of the 20 Labour MPs who publicly declared for peace in the press later in the year.[25] In the midst of all this, in 1935, the Council refused to countenance the spending of ratepayers' money to support the celebrations for King George V's Silver Jubilee, a decision lampooned in the national press.

The reputation of 'Red Nelson' depended not only on the stance of the Labour Party itself, which, in truth, especially on financial matters, had a tradition of cautious management. It was acquired also because of the activities of left-wing socialist groups which operated in and around the labour movement as a whole. The ILP was still very lively in Nelson in the inter-war years, its headquarters in Vernon Street a centre of vibrant political debate. The ILP's role as a ginger group in the town was shared with the successor organisation to the pre-war SDF – the Communist Party of Great Britain, founded just after the First World War at a time of revolutionary ferment in some parts of Britain. Zeph Hutchinson, a militant member of the NWA and later secretary of the Bacup Weavers' Association, had identified Nelson at

NELSON 1935: "I See No Signal"

6.3 The progressive politics of Nelson's Labour-controlled Municipal Council are
pilloried here in the Manchester-based *Daily Dispatch*. At the time of the celebrations
to mark George V's Silver Jubilee in 1935, the Council refused to spend public money
on such events in Nelson, preferring to provide free dinners for schoolchildren and the
unemployed. The Council even threatened (though did not actually carry it through)
not to give its employees the customary day off to mark such occasions. Though the
Council's stance was not universally applauded in Nelson, the town did have a history
of truculence when it came to relations with aristocrats and authority which went
back to the radicalism of the nineteenth century. It is also likely that many Nelsonians
took some pleasure in this image of their town as a place apart, not conforming to
the rest of the country. (*Lancashire Library, Nelson Local Studies Collection*)

this time as a 'revolutionary centre',[26] one of the places where new
left-wing politics might find succour.

However, the question of how far communism really shaped Nelson's
political development and contributed to its 'red' reputation is a problematical one. To be sure, employers, press and even county trade-union
leaders were apt to explain Nelson's militancy in terms of the influence
wielded by 'communists' and 'socialists'. In practice, however, the power
of both strands of the left was limited. The *Leader* made much of
communist activity in fomenting the conflict of 1928, for example, but
only two members of the Weavers' Committee were communists. One
of them, Seth Sagar, had a long involvement in Nelson politics which
went back to SDF days. He was an organiser of the National Unemployed Workers' Movement, a body sponsored by the CPGB, which
prompted various interventions in Nelson politics during the 1930s.
Sagar figured alongside another local communist, Elliott Ratcliffe, and

6.4 Marching for peace in the 1930s. Anti-war movements gained a sympathetic ear in Nelson, encouraged by both the Council and the Labour MP Sydney Silverman. The Labour-controlled Council had resisted central government demands that local authorities institute civil defence measures in the later 1930s. Nelson's geographical remoteness and its lack of strategic war industries meant that the town was spared aerial bombing in the war of 1939–45. (*Documentary Photography Archive, Manchester*)

the secretary of the Weavers' Association, Carey Hargreaves (not a communist), in a 'watching and besetting' case brought by the police in 1931 as a result of the demonstrations against Haighton's mill. He took the lead in attacking Arthur Greenwood, who, as Minister of Health in Ramsay MacDonald's Cabinet, was a representative of a government which the CPGB had castigated as the third capitalist party. Sagar formed part of an able cadre of communists who operated in the Nelson and Burnley area and which included women like Rose Smith, Bessie Dickinson – herself imprisoned for three months with her husband Harold on 'watching and besetting' charges – and the two weavers Maggie Chapman and Elizabeth Stanworth. They were especially articulate on women's issues such as the anomalies legislation of 1931, the effects of the 'more looms' system, and the means test, over which Sagar unsuccessfully proposed that the NWA take strike action in early 1932. Considering the energy of these people, it would be foolish to suggest that the communists had no influence; taking their cue from SDF tactics in the district a quarter of a century previously, they espoused issues of real concern to working people and tried not to become too entangled in theoretical manoeuvrings. For much of the time, however, their activities proceeded without the formal support of the Labour Party. All that the CPGB could hope to secure was the approval and occasional co-operation of Labour dissidents, one of whom was increasingly the old campaigner Selina Cooper. By the late 1930s she had developed close contacts with communists over foreign policy and the 'No More War' movement, especially after the CP itself had shed its hostility to social-democratic parties and had attempted to promote the idea of a popular front against fascism. After the anti-war demonstration of August 1934, Mrs Cooper participated in a communist-inspired visit to Nazi Germany along with Monica Whatley of Women against War and Fascism. They lobbied politicians and visited women in concentration camps. It was this increasing liaison with the communist left in the anti-war campaign that was eventually responsible for Selina Cooper's ejection from the Labour Party in 1940. Following her support for D. N. Pritt's People's Convention, a body inspired by the CPGB which made an ill-judged plea for friendship with the USSR at the time of the Nazi–Soviet non-aggression pact, the local Labour Party decided that she and a few others could no longer be tolerated for their criticisms of the government's war aims, which had the support of Labour members of the wartime coalition.[27] Even after this, however, the CP continued to work its influence. After the Nazi invasion of Russia in 1941, the party's pro-Soviet outlook became aligned with offical government policy and communist ideas were, to some extent, brought into the mainstream. In 1944, for example, the communist Harold Dickinson, as a weavers' representative on the Nelson Labour Party Executive, was able to secure a unanimous resolution condemning the action of the British government in Greece.[28] But occasional triumphs of this kind could not conceal the fact that the CPGB had long since failed to capture the Labour Party and, as a consequence, was consigned to the periphery of politics.

Nelson was therefore typical of CPGB politics in the country generally at this time. Communism was a minority movement, albeit an active one, which needed the Labour Party more than the Labour Party needed communism. In Nelson, Labour was capable of providing its own distinctive socialist culture and ideology without slipping back into the moderate, right-wing Labour stance, based on trade-unionism, often found in mining districts. For this, the Labour Party owed much to the contribution of the ILP. It was the ILP that had ensured, since before the First World War, that Labour in Nelson became something more than simply an electoral machine for sending trade union candidates to the local Council or Parliament. It was responsible for providing a channel for individual membership of the Labour Party, helping among other things, to bring many women into politics. Possibly a third of its membership in 1914 were women.[29] It also fashioned a socialist culture which, in the true Blatchfordian spirit of the *Clarion*, provided entertainment, enjoyment and recreation for politically minded people.[30] Blatchford's legacy ensured that socialist politics were as much to do with the nurturing of good comradeship and moral commitment as with electoral decision-making in smoke-filled rooms. Ideologically, the ILP had elaborated a brand of non-Marxist socialism which was based on the idea of the redistribution of wealth through the agency of the local and national state. In many ways, Nelson's Labour Town Council of the 1930s served as a working model of these ideas. The ILP's influence on Labour politics was usually, until the 1930s, a strong one. For example, its long campaign against Albert Smith's pro-war views was almost successful in 1919, when R. J. Davies was all but selected as the candidate for Nelson and Colne in preference to Smith. Smith's resignation the following year was partly caused by ILP opposition. The choice of the socialist Arthur Greenwood in 1922, against a strong field of trade-union nominees, as Labour's candidate for the constituency was largely determined by the ILP's influence at this time amongst the Nelson weavers. This probably represented the pinnacle of ILPism in Nelson, the reaping of a harvest sown before the war. The ILP's influence waned over the following decade as political conditions changed. By the early 1930s the ILP was facing, both locally and nationally, a series of problems.

To begin with, it was now the victim of its own earlier success. The more the ILP contributed to Labour's persona as a party, the less Labour came to rely on the separate ILP. This was precisely the case in Nelson. By the 1930s the Labour Party was able to sustain its political and cultural momentum without relying, as it once had, on the ILP's nerve centre at Vernon Street to generate ideas.[31] Furthermore, the rise of the Communist Party provided the ILP with a serious rival for left-wing initiatives which took some influence away from the older party. More important still for the ILP was its own relationship with the Labour Party. The problems encountered by the two Labour governments of 1924 and 1929–31, and Ramsay MacDonald's fatal decision of 1931 to form the National Government, caused many ILPers to question the appropriateness of the Labour Party as a vehicle for socialism. The fundamental problem was highlighted in the actions of Philip Snowden as Labour's Chancellor of the Exchequer. Snowden, the archetypal ILP activist of the old days, proved to be a very orthodox Chancellor. He confronted economic problems with the classic Treasury business methods of retrenchment. He did not attempt to spend his way out of economic depression and, consequently, had no policies with which to overcome the problem of unemployment. His strategy was to restore capitalism so that, once revived, its profits could be commandeered and diverted to the benefit of the workers. It was a flawed strategy which revealed that Labour, including the ILP, had no valid theory about how socialism could be brought about. It was this issue that gradually drove a wedge between Labour and the ILP, and which was chiefly responsible for the ILP's decision in 1932 to secede from the Labour Party, ostensibly over the question of who controlled ILP Members of Parliament.

The ILP was the main loser. Nationally its membership plummeted in a remarkably short space of time and the party retreated into its hardcore districts. Nelson was one, though perhaps not the most prominent. The strength of its political community in Nelson enabled the movement to keep going. Indeed, the authors of a study of the ILP meeting place in Nelson, Clarion House, have gone so far as to place 'the mid to late 30s [as] the high water mark of activity at the Clarion House'.[32] With an increasingly ageing membership, Clarion House was able to maintain an existence into the 1980s and to attract distinguished visitors to the celebrations to mark its 70th anniversary in 1982. But it was noticeable in the 1930s that old ILP stalwarts such as Mrs Cooper were beginning to devote more time to the Labour Party and even to the Communist Party. The ILP's opposition to the war in 1939 – 'not a workers' quarrel'[33] – though consistent with its stance since the pre-1914 era, did not ensure popularity in a war whose purpose seemed much clearer than that of 1914. After this, the ILP, even in Nelson, was never again the force that it had been during the first 40 years of its existence.

It was not just local initiative that was responsible for Nelson's radicalism. Parliamentary politics also played their part. This was more evident after the First World War. Before and during it, the local MPs – David Shackleton (1902–10) and Albert Smith (1910–20), as well as Robinson Graham (1920–2), the textile workers' official from Burnley who briefly succeeded Smith – lend support to the view that the Labour Party of these years was an essentially moderate organisation whose socialist commitment was tenuous.[34] Shackleton was typical of many (indeed, most) pre-war Labour MPs who campaigned for issues of concern to trade-unionists and knew little of foreign affairs and still less of socialism. He was at home in the very effective way in which he conducted himself over the passing of the Trade Disputes Act of 1906 and the creation of Labour Exchanges five years later. He became an equally effective Labour Adviser and Permanent Secretary at the Ministry of Labour, for which work he was knighted towards the end of the war. Albert Smith, secretary of the Overlookers' Association, was cast in the same mould. As an MP his work on labour legislation in conjunction with the United Textile Factory Workers' Association was exemplary, but politically he was far removed from socialism, his beliefs drawn from the stock of Liberal and radical ideas that had been common currency in north-east Lancashire in the late nineteenth century.[35] Smith's very prominent recruiting activities during the war, his decision to join up in December 1914, and, after being invalided home, his frequent appearances as a member of the Nelson tribunal which heard

6.5 Two generations of Labour politicians. Arthur Greenwood served as MP for Nelson and Colne from 1922 until 1931. He was Minister of Health in Ramsay Mac-Donald's second Labour administration (1929–31). Greenwood was the first Labour MP for the constituency not to have close links with cotton trade-unionism. His son Anthony was MP for Rossendale after the Second World War and a leading figure in Harold Wilson's Cabinets in the 1960s. (*Lancashire Library, Nelson Local Studies Collection*)

the appeals of men against conscription, all drew the fire of the ILP, which was out for his blood at the first opportunity. The campaign to unseat Smith eventually resulted in Arthur Greenwood's election as Labour MP in the general election of 1922. Greenwood, the first MP since the creation of the Clitheroe constituency in 1885 to have no local or cotton interests, was one of a younger generation of Labour intellectuals who brought ideas into politics in a way that Shackleton and Smith never had. He was an economics lecturer who became vice-president of the Workers' Educational Association, education being one of his early specialisms.[36] He had worked for the joint Research and Information Department of the TUC and Labour Party, served as parliamentary secretary to the Minister of Health in the first Labour government and, largely on the strength of this, was made Minister of Health by MacDonald in 1929. In this capacity, he was responsible for notable legislation that introduced the idea of slum clearance and which had a major impact upon housing policy in the later 1930s. He opposed MacDonald and Snowden's unemployment cuts of 1931 and, with Henderson, Clynes, Lansbury and others, left the Cabinet, thus coming out on the side of the angels. He lost Nelson and Colne in the general election of 1931, but returned to the Commons the following year as MP for Wakefield, resuming his progress through Labour's hierarchy. His later career in the Labour Party, of which he was deputy leader from 1935 to 1945, was touched with some greatness, though perhaps, ultimately, with disappointment. The socialist guru Beatrice Webb, who once had a high opinion of him, dismissed him in March 1939 as a 'confirmed drunkard',[37] though ironically the moment by which history will probably remember him came a few months later, when on the momentous evening of 2 September, in the House of Commons, he 'spoke for England' and focused criticism of Neville Chamberlain's appeasement policy.

In Arthur Greenwood, Nelson and Colne had a national figure who put the constituency on the map. His successor as Labour MP in 1935 maintained that high profile, but as much more of a firebrand. Sydney Silverman was the son of a working-class Romanian immigrant who had arrived in Liverpool in the 1890s and set up as a credit draper. After a few years in the business, there was enough money to send Sydney to Liverpool University, where he quickly gravitated into socialist circles. He joined the No Conscription Fellowship during the war, became a conscientious objector, and spent two years in Preston gaol. Practising as a lawyer in a poor district of Liverpool in the early 1930s, he became involved in city politics, joined the Labour Party, consorted with the renowned Jack and Bessie Braddock, was elected to the City Council, and unsuccessfully contested Liverpool Exchange at a by-election. It was this event that brought Silverman to the attention of Nelson and Colne Constituency Labour Party, who selected him as their candidate in 1934 against the wishes of the Textile Trades Federation, who wanted a cotton representative. At the general election of 1935 he defeated the Independent Conservative barrister Linton Thorpe, who had been returned against Greenwood in 1931, with a majority of over 4,000, remaining Nelson and Colne's MP until his death in 1968.[38]

Silverman was in many respects the perfect choice for Nelson. His own temperament suited the stance of the labour movement there. Never an office-seeker, nor part of a charmed circle of leaders, he acquired a reputation for going 'over the top on every issue'.[39] He was a typical back-bencher who spent much time with his constituents. He was a critic of many aspects of government, particularly active on matters of unemployment in the cotton industry (the subject of his maiden speech in the Commons), conscription in the late 1930s, the foreign policy of appeasement, and the question of an alliance with the Soviet Union. In the 1950s he became a leading advocate of the Campaign for Nuclear Disarmament, but the cause to which he came to devote his main energies, and for which he was best known outside Nelson, was that of capital punishment. His lobbying on this issue was rewarded

in 1957 with the Homicide Act and, in 1965, the legislation which
suspended the death penalty for five years. Permanent abolition was
effected in 1969, a year after Silverman's death.

So is the term 'Red Nelson' justified? First, we need to consider what
it might mean. A number of places attracted the label 'Little Moscow'
in the interwar period. This usually implied a strong commitment to
left-wing politics – invariably represented by the Communist Party –
based on a keen sense of working-class solidarity. Though Nelson
possessed the latter, it clearly did not have the communist dominance
in its local politics to lend credibility to the 'Moscow' epithet. There
was never the monolithic insistence on economically determined Marxism in Nelson's political clubs that would have been expressed and
disseminated in the political culture of communist towns and villages.
Ideologically, Nelson's labour philosophy was compounded of intellectual strands that had little to do with communism or Marxism. One
strand, indeed, had its origins in Nelson's Liberal past, a form of
municipal collectivism which came about because of the absence of any
leading paternalist in the district. One might suppose that this form of
politics would have been represented in Nelson no matter which party
was in control of the Council. As it was, Labour emerged as the
dominant party from the late 1920s, mobilising policies which owed
something to the thinking of their early days, when the party itself was
not socialist and still had some connections with Liberalism. In the
intervening years, however, Labour had acquired its own distinctive
ideology. This owed much to the ILP and, after 1918, to Labour's
national organisation and the electoral ideas that it generated. Thus
the municipal socialism of the late 1920s had progressed beyond such
practical issues of the early 1900s as gas meter rents and fair contracts,
but the progression was one characterised by evolution rather than by
dramatic changes. There were still similarities to be traced. Labour's
municipal socialism was premised upon strong moral commitments,
typical of the ILP and even of the chapel, to do with notions of fairness,
equality and justice. Late nineteenth-century radicals could still have
related to it in a way that they could not have related to what passed
for Marxism in the CPGB.

This helps to explain an interesting feature of Nelson's interwar
politics. The return to power of the Labour Party in 1927 was the
prelude to a rapid ascendancy. By the early 1930s it was apparent that
the party had achieved an unassailable position in the municipality. In
1931 Liberal and Conservative forces responded forming an anti-
socialist alliance which took seven of the eight seats contested that year.
The result was undoubtedly influenced by the earlier general election
success of the National Government, but it was not sustained. None
of the seven anti-socialist candidates was successful in 1933, and only

6.6 The only breach in Nelson's radical parliamentary history before the Second World War came in the general election of 1931, when barrister Linton Thorpe took Nelson and Colne as an Independent Conservative from Labour's Arthur Greenwood with a majority of over 7,000. It provided a brief period of solace for Conservatism. After 1927, there was little prospect of a non-Labour local council in Nelson, and in 1935 Sydney Silverman won the parliamentary constituency back for Labour. (*Lancashire Library, Nelson Local Studies Collection*)

one of the seven put forward in 1934 was returned. Nevertheless, these developments revealed a degree of formal co-operation between the opposition parties which had been dimly perceptible in the early years of the century, after the initial signs of the rise of Labour as a political force. What is equally interesting in the construction of this coalition, however, is the tenor of its ideological challenge to Labour's position. In short, there was none. In other words, anti-socialists attacked Labour on matters of personal experience and judgement, but not over the fundamental issue of the role of the municipality in politics. Interventionism in housing, welfare and education was accepted. Anti-socialists concentrated on the manner of political leadership rather than its substance, offering themselves to the electorate as 'administrators' rather than 'politicians', for example, and levelling charges against Labour for a lack of business expertise. It was 'socialist extravagance and maladministration' that constituted Labour's main offence, not so much socialism itself. At times, even a constitutionalist card was played to suggest that Labour's dominance of the Council and all its committees was not 'healthy': 'That town is best governed', claimed the *Leader*, 'which has a healthy, virile public opinion; in which men of all parties and of none, share in its management.'[40] Whether this argument would have been accepted had the political roles been reversed is an open question. Management, then, rather than principles, was the issue in politics at this time, and it is perhaps not too fanciful to see Nelson as an early example of the political 'consensus' that some historians have claimed to exist in British political life in the 1950s and 1960s. It was a consensus based on broad agreement in the leading political circles about the functions of the state in social and economic life – with an agreement that attention to the provision of welfare for the community was not only morally desirable but also electorally expedient. This certainly seems to have been the case in Nelson in the 1930s, and places an emphasis on continuity and moderation in the town's politics rather than extremism. All the parties had, in one sense, emerged from the same beginnings.

If this is the case, why did the label 'Red Nelson' stick? The answer is that it stemmed from activities which were either on the surface of politics or not to do with politics at all. The industrial militancy of Nelson, for example, so pronounced in the late 1920s and 1930s, had more to do with a situation than a particular political commitment. Industrial action is possible where strong trade-unionism exists; it has been evident in many places irrespective of the degree of left-wing allegiance. Though opponents of trade unions might like to attribute mass action to the machinations of tightly knit groups of politically motivated men, this is rarely an adequate explanation for the existence of strikes and lockouts. As far as Nelson is concerned, the events of 1928 and 1931–2 might well have been independent of the town's political complexion. They had little to do with whether the town was 'red'.

Nevertheless, there was something exceptional about Nelson's political behaviour. The battles with the state over the means test, the resistance to civil defence, and even the refusal to spend ratepayers' money on the king's Silver Jubilee – all attracted attention to Nelson as a place which took a stand on 'causes'. This sense of commitment had much to do with the ethical issues which, as we shall see in Chapter 7, formed an important part of the culture of both chapels and political clubs. The latter in particular nurtured a way of life that offered alternatives to capitalist society, especially in its recreational forms. Many members were predisposed to heroic political gestures and had a strong sense of politics as an arena in which moral positions were taken. This gave Nelson's politics a distinctive quality in the interwar years. But the insistence on saying what was right, rather than what was expected, the refusal to bow the knee to authority, in whatever form, was not necessarily a characteristic of the socialist left. It was just as much a part of the old Radical culture of the nineteenth-century cottage weaver who voted for Mr Gladstone because he despised men with titles. Some of this survived into twentieth-century Nelson, with the ILP's political ideologies grafted on to it. 'Red' Nelson was a mixture of these various traditions.

7

Culture and Community
between the Wars

> One felt that if all the moral agencies of the town could be brought
> together for such a purpose as this [the Peace Celebrations of 1919],
> why not on greater issues? [1]

Important though industrial and political conflict was in Nelson's development we must be wary of allowing images of discord to colour
our vision of the town. As we saw in Chapter 3, there is a sense in
which Nelson can be viewed as a united community. In direct contrast
to the industrial confrontations of 1928 and 1931–2 were occasions of
civic solidarity, when an idea of 'Nelson', and of what this meant to
people, was very clearly present. Such occasions were to be encountered
in the 1930s when Nelson Cricket Club won the Lancashire League
Championship, an achievement no less worthy of rejoicing because of
the fact that it happened rather frequently at this time. These represent
the two contradictory sides of the idea of community in Nelson. On
the one hand, a strong working-class consciousness expressed through
trade-unionism and the Labour Party and infused with a keen sense of
difference between capital and labour; on the other, an idea of Nelson
as a place in which all manner of people could find a common identity
as citizens of their town.

This sense of common identity had been real enough before the
First World War, but the war had seemed to accentuate the element
of conflict in the town's psyche. In this respect, Nelson was different
from those places where the war fostered civic cohesion. In Nelson it
provoked disagreement from beginning to end. There was no doubt
about the extent of enthusiasm for the war, as the early recruitment
figures clearly showed. Moreover, the number of Nelson men killed in
the war, though estimates are only rough, probably came close to 1,000.[2]
There was, therefore, no sense in which the town could be said to have
escaped lightly. However, Nelson had no particular military associations
or traditions. There was no equivalent to the 'Pals' battalions that were
formed in neighbouring communities in the early phases of the war,
when the system of voluntary recruitment exploited a sense of locality
to draw men into the new armies. Indeed, the opposite was in evidence.

Nelson, as we have seen, became something of a byword for opposition
to the war, a centre in which conscientious objectors might find succour.
There was certainly little of the civic commitment to the war that was
to be found in nearby Bury, the home of the Lancashire Fusiliers and
a town which supplied many of its men for the disastrous campaign at
Gallipoli in 1915.[3] Nor does Nelson as a community seem to have been
psychologically affected by the war in the same way as Bury, where the
scars of the 1914–18 conflict, and the 'human wreckage'[4] created by
it, wrought an influence on the town for years to come. The impact
of the war in Nelson was much more ambiguous. It was symbolised in
some ways by the rather bewildered state of mind that greeted the news
of the end of hostilities: 'the streets were crowded with people in the
afternoon … there was nothing for them to do and they wandered
aimlessly to and fro in vain expectation of a meeting or demonstration.'[5]
People expected an official event, but none happened. The crowds were
'sober and thoughtful', far less boisterous than they had been at the
end of the South African War 16 years earlier. In fact, when some
people attempted to enforce a holiday by preventing others from going
into work, ugly scenes developed. They prompted the *Leader* to de-
nounce this behaviour as a manifestation of the kind of spirit that the
War had been fought to put an end to.[6]

The *Leader* was aware that Nelson had acquired a reputation for
conflict – a town of 'many disruptive elements', according to the
newspaper.[7] It was gratified, therefore, to perceive in the official peace
celebrations, held in August 1919, a demonstraton of something more
positive – Nelson's community spirit. The peace celebrations, staged
in and around the cricket field from Sunday 3 August to Tuesday 5
August 1919, were part of a national scheme to celebrate the end of
the war. The date had been fixed nationally for 19 July, but this clashed
with Nelson holdays. In Nelson, therefore, the celebrations were sched-
uled for early August. As far as was possible with such events, they
were conducted in Nelson in a moderate way. There was certainly no
attempt made to glorify war or to indulge in maudlin sentiments. The
mayor, Alderman Rickard, opened the proceedings with some emotional
words about the fallen; he then went on, in a rather odd vein, to attempt
to rationalise the war as a sacrifice that 'would help to cleanse, to purify
and purge the nation'. Aside from this, however, the celebrations were
soberly managed, in a form similar to that of Charter Day, with a long
procession on the Monday which embraced most of the leading organisations in the town. Though it contained a march past by discharged
soldiers, who were entertained afterwards to a free lunch in a large
marquee in Victoria Park, there was a conspicuous absence of any
military presence. Indeed, emphasis was placed on children, with Sunday
school groups strongly in evidence, and on the elderly, for whom special
events were arranged on the Tuesday. The various religious denomi-

7.1 Reedyford Hospital, shortly after it had been converted to its medical role during the First World War. The house had formerly been the home of William Tunstill, who died in 1903. Reedyford Hospital became a symbol of local voluntarism between the wars, the subject of many fund-raising events. In spite of Nelson's reputation for its municipal social services in the interwar period, Reedyford Hospital was not incorporated into the local state health system. It eventually became an NHS hospital. Its foundations now lie under the M65 motorway. (*Lancashire Library, Nelson Local Studies Collection*)

nations were prominent throughout, especially at the very beginning of the celebrations, when all Nelson's choirs assembled in front of the cricket pavilion to sing sacred music. As an event to celebrate the end of the war, it was characterised, considering the circumstances of the time, by good taste and sensibility. The *Leader's* hope that the physical unity of the borough, as embodied in the celebrations, might be maintained thereafter was a pious one, but nonetheless the events did reveal something of the spirit of Nelson.[8] So, too, did an idea that had emerged shortly before this to express 'remembrance' in the form of a hospital, a practical rather than a symbolic gesture. Reedyford Hospital was the result, which perhaps explains why it became such a focus of civic patriotism between the wars.[9] Nelson was conspicuously absent from the vogue in the early 1920s to erect public war memorials.

Such things could override diversity at times, but the multiple allegiances in Nelson's social fabric still remained, and could still generate hostilities. In many ways, Nelson was the archetypal proletarian community. The designation 'Little Moscow', which came into use (at least among newspaper reporters) in the late 1920s, derived as much from the culture of socialism that was embedded in Nelson as from the formal political and industrial organisation of labour. By the 1930s a number of clubs and associations provided a way of life which was based upon socialist precepts and which, therefore, presented a challenge to the ethic of capitalism prevalent in society at large. Though the British socialist movement was noticeably less successful than some of its European counterparts – particularly the German – in establishing an 'alternative culture',[10] there were nonetheless pockets of socialist fellowship in Britain every bit as vibrant as those to be found in continental Europe. Nelson was one place where such a culture could be found.

Alongside the Weavers' Institute, which in many senses acted as the hub of the labour movement, a number of other organisations performed social and cultural functions. The ILP, with its headquarters in Vernon Street, was more than a political organisation. Since its inception in the early 1890s, the ILP had always contained an influential body of opinion which argued that the party existed as much to make socialists as to contest elections. Educational and recreational activity was therefore an essential part of its operation. Nelson ILP held fast to this principle. In addition to a regular programme of classes and discussion groups on the leading political and economic issues of the day, it laid on more mundane activities, such as weekly whist drives and classes in 'physical culture', which included boxing, weightlifting and wrestling. Associated with the ILP and also holding its meetings at Vernon Street was the Socialist Sunday school. It offered a secular alternative to the many chapel- and church-based Sunday schools. Children would sing 'hymns' from the *Socialist Sunday School Hymn Book*, play games to musical accompaniment, and have lessons – 'we settled into our classes ... and sit in a little circle round our teachers'. The school was also well known for its football team, which participated in local competitions. Taking an idea from the Labour Church movement, which had been popular in some areas before the war, the Sunday school had 'baptisms' at which children were given middle names associated with a leading figure in the labour movement. Part of the same network of organisations around the ILP was the Clarion Cycling Club, an association inspired by the immensely popular pre-war socialist newspaper, the *Clarion*, edited by Robert Blatchford. Blatchford had always believed that socialism was something to be enjoyed and cycling was one of the most popular pursuits taken up by socialists in the North of England. Nelson Clarion Club organised weekly runs of varying degrees of difficulty throughout the interwar years, usually into the Yorkshire Dales or the Trough of Bowland. Energies were not confined to cycling, however. The club campaigned vigorously against a series of official measures – cycle tracks, rear lights and the cycle tax – which were regarded as unwarranted intrusions into the freedom of the road. Even the old SDF, for so long on the margins of the labour movement and much diminished in size and influence since its peak in the 1890s, maintained an independent existence in its premises in Ann Street, where regular tea parties and concerts were held in the interwar years. Such activities provided a culture of good fellowship based upon upright and healthy enjoyment which brought together people of similar persuasions in a comradely spirit. They formed an important underpinning to labour solidarity in the town.[11]

By the 1930s, however, the role of such activities was diminishing in importance as the Labour Party itself consolidated a cultural base. Nelson Labour Party was active in a variety of cultural provision – the Nelson Socialist Dramatic Society being a leading example – but equally important was the development of neighbourhood events organised by the ward committees. The social and dance at the Co-op Room in Clover Hill Road in January 1928 was typical of this kind of event, combining entertainment with bringing political consciousness to the people. Joint ventures would be staged on occasion, such as the All Star Variety Show, produced by Nelson Labour Party and Bradley ward in March 1938, featuring Jack Brown and his cabaret with Learie Constantine in the chair. A good evening's entertainment was had for 6d. (2½p) – reduced price for children. Of particular importance in Labour social events was the Women's Section, responsible for organising several activities of varying levels of ambition. They ranged from the Grand Fancy Dress Carnival, held at the Weavers' Institute just after New Year 1928 and judged by the MP for Nelson and Colne, Arthur Greenwood, to the more regular and modest gatherings and 'at homes' at which political and social issues were discussed over a cup of tea. The Women's Section was a forum not only for maintaining women's support for Labour at this time, but also for ensuring that feminist issues were presented in the party's ideology.[12]

Equally significant in accounting for the development of socialist culture was the Co-operative Society. Through its Educational Department, it continued its pre-war custom of organising a series of informative but not excessively highbrow lectures and talks at the Co-operative Hall in Albert Street. 'Tramps in Lakeland' and 'In Search of the Sparrowhawk' were two typical offerings, reflecting a popular and perennial rural interest which was also given attention by the Fellowship Rambles arranged by the department. Alongside these activites were the events promoted by the Excursions Department. For Nelson Holidays in 1929, for instance, the Co-op offered, for £7 17s. 6d. (£7.85) a conducted tour to Ilfracombe 'Land of Sunshine, Junket and Cream, Star of the Severn Sea', and an even more adventurous tour to Belgium, which was promised to be 'the best tour that has ever left Nelson for the Continent'. More controversial was the Education Department's promotion of sex education, a topic pioneered by Selina Cooper in the 1920s. In December 1930, for example, the Co-op started a series of lectures 'Sex – what it is and what it means', reinforcing the emphasis given to questions of maternity and birth control in municipal social services.[13]

Such activities had manifold purposes and effects, from electioneering to fund-raising, keeping supporters together, providing pleasure of a mental or physical kind and, as in the case of sex education, conveying much-needed information. But, no matter how simple their nature, they were morally uplifting activities of a creative kind. They did not depend upon entertainment in a ready-made form. While it would be wrong to suggest that socialist culture of this sort contested the institutions and ethics of capitalism at every turn, it did nonetheless serve to inspire a sense of togetherness in a distinctive way of life. It was therefore one of the many elements that contributed to Nelson's notion of itself as being 'special'.

In this respect, the institutions of the labour and socialist movement were adapting a tradition established earlier by both secular and religious organisations. One aspect of working-class self-help in leisure can be found in the allotment movement, which had grown up since the Allotment Act of 1894. By the 1920s it was a well-supported and, at times, politically influential group which drew in a mixture of different people. Motives for acquiring an allotment varied. Some saw it as a resource which would supplement the domestic economy and even supply marketable produce. This consideration affected unemployed workers in particular in the 1930s, though they had to be careful that any surplus did not come into the means test. More usually, however, the allotment was seen by factory workers as an opportunity to be out in the fresh air after a day in the mill. There was a 'back to nature' element about allotment holding for many people, whose houses, it should be remembered, did not usually have gardens. The sociability of the allotments was also valued. They provided a place where friendships could be formed and maintained. Pride was also taken in the quality of the produce, displayed at the annual flower show organised by the Nelson and District Smallholders, Allotments and Horticultural Association each September. This occasion also provided the opportunity for generating an element of civic pride, as prizes were offered for the best-kept gardens in municipal properties. Moreover, in spite of the literary stereotype of the allotment as a place of male sanctuary, Nelson allotments seem to have been places where the sexes mixed freely, to be expected maybe in a town where gender equality was the norm. All these factors explain the solidarity that was displayed by the movement when allotments were threatened by repossessions for house or road building. In the 1920s, for example, the Allotment Society took the Town Council to court in an attempt to preserve land for cultivation, and a decade later the society successfully threatened political action in the municipal elections, forcing the

7.2 Two aspects of Nelson society in the 1930s. Meredith Street (above) – a little enclave of 'better off' housing – was the home of Learie Constantine. Just around the corner was Vernon Street (right), where the Socialist Institute housed ILP meetings and kept a flourishing left-wing political culture alive well into the post-Second World War era.

Labour-controlled Council to withdraw a plan to repossess land for fear of losing allotment holders' votes.[14]

Religious activities were still carried on alongside the purely secular ones. By the 1930s, however, their influence was on the wane as a consequence both of the influence of labour and socialism and the more commercialised pleasures that were beginning to develop. The decline was recognised by the churches themselves. In the 1920s and 1930s many groups that had been established in the 1860s and 1870s were celebrating landmarks in their development, organising Jubilee bazaars and other events to commemorate 50 or more years of activity. There was a certain amount of irony in the fact that these events often served to highlight the decline of religion since its heyday in the years before the First World War. The Stanley Street Methodists, for example, dated back to 1865 and had built a handsome Italianate chapel, seating over 600 people, in 1886 at a cost of over £3,000. By the time of their Jubilee bazaar in 1936 they were complaining that 'In common with many Churches, we suffer from depleted congregations. This means reduced income ... our premises need renovating ... we urgently need £650 to free us of our current debt.'[15] This theme was prominent in most of the commemorative events which took place in these years. 'Sunday by Sunday', wrote the author of the Temple Street Methodists' Jubilee handbook of 1946, 'the preacher has been confronted with rows of empty seats. Indeed, there have been times when the congregation has found a large classroom sufficient for its needs.'[16] But the various branches of the nonconformist movement could still exercise a cultural role. Carr Road Methodists and Salem Chapel could aspire to rival the Weavers' Institute as a nerve centre, and Manchester Road Congregationalists experienced a revival of their fortunes in the mid-1920s with the arrival of A. E. Hill as minister. At their Jubilee celebrations in 1935 the famous organist Reginald Dixon from Blackpool played in the festival of music, which was broadcast in the BBC's Northern Region. Each week in the 1920s the front page of the *Leader* was packed with details of whist drives, dances, musical services, concerts, recitals, potato pie suppers, jumble sales and lantern lectures organised by the abundance of nonconformist chapels.[17] Music featured prominently in the attractions of these events. The choral tradition was strong in Nelson, and local choirs achieved recognition for the town by their successes in national competitions. The Nelson Arion and the Barrowford Glee Union were both renowned groups, only slightly outshone by the Nelson Excelsior Glee Union, a choir which had its origins in the Zion Baptist Glee Union before the First World War.[18] But this was only one side of religious life. Like the labour organisations, Nonconformity often framed its cultural activities in a clear political context. When the Independent Methodists held their 126th annual conference in Nelson over four days in June 1931, there was a strong political theme in the agenda: the international economy, the Indian question, unemployment, and disarmament were all topics to be confronted. Mr George Hunter of Leigh presided over a large public session and his opening remarks neatly illustrate how closely interwoven religion and politics were:

> there was no subject that belonged more to the church than peace ... If their Saviour was upon the earth he wondered where He would be going? He thought He would be going to Geneva, where he hoped by the guidance of the Spirit of God and the highest principles of justice and equity between nations, the matter of war would be settled. He knew that a great many prominent men in the country would have to retrace their steps if war was to be avoided. Bishops would have to cease blessing battleships. (Applause).[19]

The cultural influences issuing from these sources provided a link from which the local community of club or chapel could be merged into a civic identity of Nelson. If, however, we move from this sphere of voluntary provision of culture to the more commercialised world of leisure, we find influences that place Nelson in a growing international arena. Commercial popular culture, often frowned upon by socialists and nonconformists alike, but for different reasons, had relatively little scope for development in a town the size of Nelson before the Second World War. The consumer market was limited by earning power, and an associational 'do-it-yourself' lifestyle was already established. But commercial leisure did have its attractions, especially in the shape of the 'pictures'.

An innovative form of entertainment dating from before the war, cinema perpetuated influences that had developed even earlier. It owed much to the traditions of music hall, an institution which does not appear to have been implanted very firmly in Nelson. Repertory theatre of a more serious kind was well represented before and after the advent of cinema at the Palace Theatre in Leeds Road and also at the Tivoli, home of the Nelson Players.[20] Closer links to cinema as an entertainment genre in Nelson terms could have been the result of behaviour and ideas gleaned from holidays in Blackpool. The Lancashire seaside resort so beloved of Nelsonians, with its piers, pleasure beach and Golden Mile, represented a devotion to modern pleasure which drew extensively upon American inspiration. The cinema came foursquare in this tradition. In the early 1920s, when Nelson cinema-goers had a choice of some six picture houses, ranging from the 'super' establishments like the Palace or the Electric Palace in the town centre to the smaller Palace in Barrowford, the British film industry was still competing with the American challenge and there was generally an even balance between domestic and imported films.[21] As the costs of both film and cinema production rose, however, especially with the introduction of 'talkies' in 1929, British companies found it more difficult to compete with the American product, already assured of its own vast domestic market as a guaranteed source of profit. In fact, Parliament introduced an element of protection for the British cinema industry in 1928 with the application of the 'quota' system, which required that a proportion of all films shown should be British. This did not always please the distributors and picture-house owners, whose chief concern was to show the films that audiences wanted to see, irrespective of their country of origin. Nevertheless, by the 1930s there was a preponderance of American films on display, with stars like Clark Gable, Bebe Daniels and Gary Cooper. Nelson's major cinemas, seven by now, all boasted the Western Electric Sound System and staged double features, often with a change of programme midway through the week. The cinema was undoubtedly a popular pastime and was frequently aimed specifically at women: the 'woman's film', a typical example from the 1920s being *The Outcast*, starring Gladys Brockwell – 'the superb appeal of a Mother's fight for her child, her honour, and her home ... a picture every mother should see' – was a regular feature of cinema-going in the interwar years. The pictures took people, whether women, families or courting couples, out of Nelson and into a vision of the world constructed in Hollywood, USA.

Other commercial entertainments were also beginning to make their mark in these years. Notable among them, for younger people, was the ballroom dancing craze, principally catered for in Nelson at the Imperial in Carr Road. For 6*d.* (2½p) midweek or 1*s.* (5p) on Saturdays an evening dancing to all the popular tunes of the day could be had, performed by Cliff Bateson's or Frank Brindle's 'New Imperials'. It was at about this time in British society that a generational division in cultural taste began to emerge, prefiguring the 'teenage' phenomenon of the 1950s. One imagines that age largely determined the choice between, on the one hand, an evening at the Imperial or Ritz ballrooms and, on the other, the summer concerts in the park sponsored by the Town Council and featuring the Nelson Symphony Orchestra.[22]

Insofar as cultural and recreational activities served to create a sense of local community there was one pastime which, arguably, contributed more than any other to this process: sport. Many of the rural sports that immigrants had brought with them into Nelson were dying out by the interwar years, replaced by pastimes more suitable for an urban environment. Knur and spell, for example, continued to be played, sometimes to large gatherings of people who turned up to watch the game's champion, Billy Baxter of Colne, but increasingly sports like this were kept going by a small minority of enthusiasts.[23] Likewise, events such as 'Nick o'Thung's Charity', a Barrowford activity created in the 1850s as an annual mass picnic to Pendle on the first Sunday in

7.3 Knur and spell – 'poor man's golf' – played downwind on open ground. The field of play was marked out in 20-yard divisions, and the winner was whoever had the biggest aggregate total of hits, measured in scores of yards, after an agreed number of strikes. It needed plenty of room, and the countryside around Nelson afforded ample opportunity for the playing of this old game. Its survival is evidence that old forms of recreation can exist alongside newer sports like football and cricket. In fact, Jerry Dawson, goalkeeper for Burnley both before and after the First World War, was one of the district's champion players. One of the chief attractions for spectators was betting on the outcome and, as late as 1970, a match near Elland, Yorkshire, involving the Colne champion, Greenfield, was attended by some 3,000 spectators. (*Lancashire Library, Nelson Local Studies Collection*)

May, which might actually have been a cover for the illegal male sport of cock-fighting, were maintained after the war as a reminder of an older form of recreation.[24] For most Nelsonians, however, sport, by the 1920s, usually meant football and cricket. The town and its outlying districts were honeycombed with a multitude of clubs based on churches, chapels, Sunday schools, political organisations, mills and neighbourhoods. To win a local competition, as Barrowford St Thomas's did in 1932, when they headed the Nelson and District Sunday School League, was not only a signal achievement in the lives of many young men, but an important way of registering identity. But it was to the clubs that carried the name of the town that people looked most often for the fulfilment of a civic identity through sport.

The name of Nelson was put on the map, so to speak, in a dramatic way by the early success of Nelson Football Club (FC) in the newly enlarged Football League of the early 1920s. The club, founded in the early 1880s, had done well in Lancashire leagues and joined the Third

7.4 All smiles for Nelson Football Club in 1923, when the club had just won promotion to the Second Division of the Football League only two seasons after joining. Disappointments soon followed, however. Nelson was too small to sustain hopes of continued league success, and the club lost its national league status in 1931, returning to the regional competition from which it had arisen. Seated front (fifth left) is the popular goalscorer Joe Eddleston, later of Swindon Town, Hull City and manager of Reading. His son Maurice, himself a talented amateur player for Reading and England, later became a well-known radio sports broadcaster. (*Lancashire Library, Nelson Local Studies Collection*)

Division (North) when it was created in 1921. Nelson were promoted in only their second season, though their first spell in the Second Division (1923–4) proved to be their last. They lost nearly half of their matches and finished second to bottom, in front of Bristol City. Returning to the Third Division for 1924–5 the club rallied and finished second to Darlington, though this placement did not bring them promotion. There followed a couple of respectable seasons until, in 1927–8, they conceded a record 136 goals. After this, Nelson never rose beyond the bottom half of the division. They failed to secure re-election in 1931 (local legend, more myth than reality, maintained that Burnley, themselves struggling in the Second Division by this time, voted against them) and were replaced in the league by Chester.

Nelson FC's problems stemmed mainly from a shortage of funds. In spite of the strenuous efforts of the Supporters' Club to raise money by organising dances, whist drives and socials, they never realised enough to ensure the sound financial footing that league football required. A sequence of poor results on the field also brought a psychology of defeat to the team. The *Nelson Gazette* thought that, by 1928, the players had developed an 'inferiority complex'.[25] At bottom, however, it was a question of attendances. Though the ground itself, Seedhill, was a fine one by lower-division standards, it was never full enough in a town the size of Nelson. Hope of the financial returns required to capture, through the transfer market, the necessary playing strength to survive was always illusory. Good players like Sam Wadsworth, Jimmy Hampson and the popular goalscorer Joe Eddleston, who went to Swindon, were sold to bigger clubs to raise money. But in spite of such windfalls, the club was heavily in debt by the early 1930s. The Town Council was a major creditor. It was owed money for unpaid water and gas bills as well as for rates. It was estimated that, at the point when Nelson FC left the league, it was in debt to the sum of £5,000.[26] There was much regret in the town at the club's disappearance from the national football scene, though expectation, buoyed by early success, had always been rather unrealistic, especially with larger clubs like Burnley and Blackburn Rovers so near. As the historians of the Football League put it: 'You can't run a big store on a small shopkeeper's capital, and you cannot run a football club long on debts and liabilities.'[27] Nelson FC illustrated the difficulties of promoting big-time professional football in a small industrial town. Its failure was frequently mirrored in similar communities such as Durham, Merthyr, South Shields, Stalybridge, Ashington and Aberdare, who all dropped out of the league during the interwar period.[28]

More successful in carrying the pride of Nelson to the outside world was the cricket team. Nelson Cricket Club (CC) was one of the original members of the Lancashire League in 1891 and, as one of the bigger clubs in the league, had always nourished expectations of success. Few of its supporters, however, would have dared to dream of the dominance that it came to enjoy in the 1930s, when the club won the championship seven times and came second twice. This success was, to a very large degree, the result of engaging the Trinidadian cricketer Learie Constantine as a professional in 1929. In some respects, though, the breakthrough can be traced back to the early 1920s, when Nelson CC made a decision that reshaped much of league cricket in the North.

Frustrated by lack of success in the years immediately following the First World War, especially in 1921, the Nelson Committee took the unprecedented step that year of signing the Australian fast bowler E. A. McDonald. This initiative, achieved after much persistence and subterfuge by committee members in the face of resistance from the Australian cricket authorities, not only secured the services of a leading international player but also captured maximum publicity for the club and town. At the time of the deal, McDonald, alongside his fast-bowling partner Jack Gregory, had been chiefly responsible for destroying the English batting in a Test series which Australia had won overwhelmingly. His signing attracted much comment from the press, national and local, not all of it complimentary. It also had an instantaneous effect in boosting Nelson CC membership subscriptions, especially

from women. McDonald's achievements on the field during the three
seasons (1922–4) that he played for Nelson were less than had been
anticipated (fast bowlers were not always helped by the slow pitches in
the league), but his impact on cricket in Lancashire was considerable.
The presence in the league of so celebrated a performer had a generally
stimulating effect upon interest, and this was reflected in match attendances. In 1925, when McDonald left Nelson to join the Lancashire
County Club in a transfer deal which among other things secured for
Nelson a series of county matches during the next few seasons, the
club secretary wrote: '[his] departure is not only a loss to Nelson but
to the whole of the Lancashire League. Every club has benefited as a
result of our enterprise in signing McDonald and he brought a new
interest and enthusiasm to the League when there was a tendency for
it to be weakening.'[29]

The McDonald episode ensured that cricket in Nelson (and, to a
large extent, in the rest of the Lancashire League) was established on
a larger footing than it had been before the First World War. This
had seemed likely even before McDonald's arrival. Comparing the
club's receipts for 1921 (£3,391) and 1914 (£706), the treasurer had
claimed that 'the Club is now a huge concern'.[30] The arrival of McDonald certainly continued this process. It also paved the way for the far
more spectacular reign of Constantine, from 1929 to 1937. These years
saw Nelson achieve a kind of dominance over Lancashire League cricket
that Arsenal produced in the Football League and Yorkshire obtained
in the County Cricket Championship. Whether in batting, bowling or
fielding – in which his exploits were almost magical, earning him the
nickname 'electric heels' – there were few heights that Constantine
failed to attain. Remembered above all, perhaps, were his 10 wickets
for 10 runs in the match against Accrington in 1934, his innings of
124, out of a score of 175, in just over an hour against Enfield in 1929,
or the remarkable total of 192 not out against East Lancashire in August
1937. Like McDonald, his presence on the field was guaranteed to raise
the gate-receipts on any ground, so much so that other clubs came to
rely upon a visit by Nelson to boost their finances. This 'Constantine
factor' became a key aspect of Lancashire League cricket in the 1930s.
The *Cricketer Annual* had observed something of the kind at the end
of Constantine's first season: 'mainly owing to the huge gates and the
magnetic influence of Constantine, together with the fine weather,
several clubs were lifted out of debt which they have carried for years:
a wonderful happening'.[31] In fact, in 1936, to mark the league's appreci-
ation of the continuing Constantine factor, the other clubs organised
a benefit match for him which raised some £500.[32] Constantine's contribution can be judged from the statistics presented in a letter to the
Leader in 1934 by Mr Crabtree, president of the Lancashire League.
His figures showed that, between 1929 and 1933, the gate-receipts at

7.5 Learie Constantine from Trinidad (on left) – 'Connie' (sometimes 'electric heels') – was Nelson's cricket professional from 1929 until 1937. During this time Nelson enjoyed an unchallenged superiority in the Lancashire League. Here club captain Harold Hargreaves is being presented with the championship cup in 1929. Constantine was described by his fellow Trinidadian, the writer C. L. R. James, as 'a League cricketer who played test cricket'. He was in many ways the ideal 'pro' – attacking batsman, devastating fast bowler, and a magician in the field – and became the town's best-known personality in the 1930s. He was made a freeman of the borough in 1963. (*Lancashire Library, Nelson Local Studies Collection*)

matches involving Nelson (one seventh of the total number of matches played in this period) amounted to £15,779 – some 75 per cent of the sum total of receipts at all matches in the period.[33]

Nelson thus became a cornerstone of league cricket in the 1930s, causing the town's reputation to be advanced. Indeed, Constantine became one of those local champions by whom a town is not only known to outsiders, but through whose prowess the town identifies itself. The special relationship that grew between Nelson and Constantine was also cultivated through activities other than sport. Constantine lived in Nelson, in Meredith Street, and continued to do so long after he had ceased playing for the club. He participated in local events, attended and spoke at meetings, and formed a circle of friends both inside and outside cricket.[34] The adulation that he received in the town was clearly expressed by a visitor from New Zealand who attended the match in 1937 at which Nelson yet again took the league title, the last occasion on which it was achieved with Constantine:

I shall never forget the scene on that famous ground when the last wicket fell. Everyone went mad, hats, sticks and caps were thrown high in the air and 'Connie' was hoisted shoulder high and carried off the field ... His personality is tremendous, wonderful ... to say that he has been a godsend to Nelson is to put it mildly. He has, to all people, both living in and out of Nelson, *been Nelson itself*.[35]

This was all the more remarkable considering that Constantine was black and, furthermore, a Roman Catholic. Indeed, he was the first black cricketer of any prominence to play in Lancashire, whether at league or county level, although success at Nelson gave rise to a series of black West Indian cricketers in the Lancashire League during the 1930s and after the Second World War. George Headley, Manny Martindale, Edwin St Hill, Ellis Achong and Everton Weekes were among the better known of a company of talented overseas players. There was, of course, in contrast with later years, no black community in Nelson at this time. Constantine's friend, the Trinidadian writer and radical C. L. R. James, claimed that when he went to Nelson in the early 1930s to stay with the Constantines, 'apart from someone who went around collecting refuse in an old pushcart, Learie and I were the only coloured men in Nelson'.[36] In spite of the racial attitudes that prevailed in Britain generally, casting black people as 'inferior' to whites, the population of Nelson had no difficulty in identifying with Constantine. Though Constantine himself claimed on one occasion that he had been the victim of some 'shots' (snubs) on account of his colour,[37] the town's radical and nonconformist traditions, emphasising equal rights and democracy, no doubt helped to foster a spirit of equality. Constantine's Catholic background, nurtured in Trinidad, does not seem to have been an obstacle to his reception in Nelson. Prejudice against Catholics (especially if Irish) was still present in the 1930s, though it was never as vitriolic here as in towns in the westerly parts of Lancashire. Local people took pride in the fact that their champion was not only a splendid cricketer but a perfect gentleman who spoke 'beautiful English', in contrast to the Lancashire accents of most others. They also drew pride from the fact that Constantine's presence reflected their tolerance as a host community. As with other 'celebrities' of the period, especially in the field of entertainment, popular prejudices against colour and religion could be suspended in individual cases. Constantine's elevated status in Nelson – indeed, the 'star' treatment that he was accorded – contrasted sharply with the position that he would have experienced in the colonial Caribbean, even as a famous cricketer: 'first-class status as a cricketer ... third-class status as a man', as C. L. R. James memorably described it.[38] He encountered outright discrimination in other parts of England also. In 1944, for example, journeying to London to play in an international cricket match, he and his family were turned out of the Imperial Hotel in Russell Square because the management had received complaints from white American servicemen about the presence of a black man in their midst.[39] Constantine repaid the affection and esteem in which he was held by Nelsonians by honouring them in later life. When the Labour government made him a life peer in 1969 he took the title Baron Constantine, of Maraval in Trinidad and Tobago, and of Nelson in the County Palatine of Lancaster.

There is, then, a very real sense in which Constantine, and the other Nelson professionals of this era – Ted McDonald, J. M. Blanckenburg and Lala Amarnath – helped to give the town of Nelson an identity. They embodied the town's hopes and pride and also connected it to a wider comunity of international proportions. When McDonald signed for Nelson in 1921, the town became a focus of interest for people as far away as Sydney, Australia.[40] It was somehow appropriate that a town whose economy had worldwide connections should be similarly placed in the sporting world.

How far the cricket club, as opposed to its star players, provided a solid focus of unity is another matter. Institutions of this type – grammar schools, hospitals and newspapers are others – are often seen as icons of local identity. But they might not always be seen in this light within the community. Nelson Cricket Club is a case in point. In some respects, it occupied an ambiguous position in the town. In one sense it attracted a wide range of people as members. Since the late nineteenth century, it had offered a number of different categories of membership, each type suited to a different pocket and each bestowing different privileges. In the 1920s, for example, one of the largest groups of members was made up of women, who could enrol for 7s. 6d. (37p) a season. In 1924 ladies' membership accounted for some 30 per cent of the total membership of almost 800, and one tenth of membership subscriptions. In this respect, the club had a broadly based composition in gender, age and class terms, and no doubt attracted a similar range of paying spectators through the turnstiles.[41] It seemed a genuinely 'open' institution. It is somewhat surprising, therefore, to find that it was the subject of criticism from some quarters for being partisan. This criticism stemmed mainly from the political left. 'Considering that it is a town's institution, non-political, non-sectarian and all the rest of it', complained the *Nelson Gazette* in 1935, 'the Nelson Cricket Club has a tendency to Liberal influence.'[42] The *Gazette* noted the Liberal sympathies of many of the club's officials, including the president, David Tattersall, a mill owner, and the chairman, T. E. Morgan, who ran the *Nelson Leader*. The real point at issue here was that business deriving from the club – printing and advertising chiefly – seemed to flow directly into the *Leader*'s office. 'But just let us suppose that the situation were reversed ... supposing all official positions of the club were occupied by leading members of the Labour Party ... there would be an outcry about political influence!' [43]

Much of this was a storm in a teacup, though the basic observation was valid. The Cricket Club did act as a focus for Liberal opinion in the inter-war years, at least within the committee. The politically ambitious Nelson solicitor J. H. S. Aitken saw fit to cultivate close links with the club in the course of campaigning for the Liberals in the Nelson and Colne constituency in the 1920s. Two leading and long-serving officials, Teddy Ashton – secretary of the club from 1913 until his death in 1932, when he was still working as a warper in a local mill – and Ben Chadwick, the club's treasurer, were both active Liberals. Chadwick stood as a municipal candidate for the anti-socialist cause in elections in the early 1930s, as did Ashton's successor as Secretary, Councillor J. H. Warburton.[44] In some senses the Cricket Club might be viewed as an alternative to the Weavers' Institute as a focus of political opinion and allegiance. Plainly, the place of sport and sporting clubs in the community carried contradictory influences, though they must still be counted among those agencies which helped to promote a sense of local patriotism.

This was never more clearly in evidence than when the Nelson club was engaged in a cricketing battle with its great rival, Colne. All Lancashire League cricket matches were local 'Derbys' in a sense, but those between Nelson and Colne attracted particular attention in the two towns. The grounds would be full well before the start of the match on these occasions, with Nelson's supporters – led by their redoubtable barracker-in-chief, Alwyn Nightingale ('Nightie') – well to the fore. On one famous occasion at the Horsefield, in Colne, Nightie was berating the Colunians over a new-fangled motor roller being used to prepare the wicket, comparing it unfavourably with the donkey that was used to pull the heavy roller at Nelson. 'What's so special about an old donkey?', asked the Colne supporters: 'it's got gold bloody teeth', replied Nightie. They were special occasions, with the crowds embodying the pride of the respective communities. A *Leader* report of one such 'Derby' in the first season after the Great War is worth quoting in some detail for the sense that it conveys of the intense communal interest in the match, to the point where almost the whole of Nelson appeared to be 'on the move' to Colne:

> The match at Colne on Saturday was an 'old-timer' in every sense of the phrase. The day could not have been more propitious. There was a bright and genial sun which radiated pleasure all round, and it was an ideal day from the spectators' point of view. The influx of Nelsonians was the greatest for many years. The [tram]cars were crowded, and if there had been another dozen cars available the Nelson and Colne Tramways Committee would have reaped a rich

7.6 Holidays at home, 1944. Wartime travel restrictions, including shortage of petrol, coastal security measures and the general need to save money encouraged the idea, which was given blessing by the government. Though Nelsonians had become accustomed to annual holidays, especially to Blackpool, since before the First World War, their cultural life afforded them plenty of opportunities for home-grown pleasure during the wartime emergency. The slow development of commercial leisure in Nelson meant that, by the early 1940s, there was still a rich seam of voluntary associational recreation, supplemented by municipal activities, which could be mined to provide 'holidays at home'. The scheme was not, however, an outstanding success. (*By permission of the British Library and the editor of the Nelson Leader*)

PUBLIC NOTICES

 BOROUGH OF NELSON.

HOLIDAYS AT HOME - 1944

PROGRAMME OF EVENTS.

Monday, 3rd July, to Friday, 7th July.

In Victoria Park:
  DONKEYS and PONIES from Bridlington.
  ROUNDABOUTS and SWINGS.
  PUNCH and JUDY.

On the Public Bowling Greens:
  BOWLING COMPETITIONS.

In various parts of the town:
  MOBILE CINEMA PERFORMANCES.

At the Cinemas:
  FREE CINEMA PERFORMANCES for elderly people—
  During the period Monday, 3rd July, to Friday, 7th July, 1944, inclusive, the Proprietors of all the Cinemas and Theatres in the Borough have agreed to admit persons 65 years of age and over to one performance at any Cinema or Theatre.
  To secure this privilege, all **persons 65 years of age and over,** residing in the Borough, **must submit their Pension Books or Birth Certificates** to the TOWN CLERK'S OFFICE, TOWN HALL, NELSON, between 9 a.m. and 6 p.m. any day except Saturday, when the hours will be 9 a.m. to 12 noon.

Tuesday, 4th July:
On the Cricket Field—at 2-0 p.m.:
  CHILDREN'S SPORTS and TEAM GAMES;
  ROBBIE HAYHURST—the World's Greatest Trick Motor Cyclist (International Champion). THRILLS WITHOUT SPILLS!!!

In Victoria Park—at 7-30 p.m. (If wet, in the Weavers' Institute):
  THE KEITH-LEA ENTERTAINERS—
  Dorothy Beckwith, Soprano;   Charles Whiteoak, Tenor;
  Florrie Whitaker, Contralto;   Leo Chapman, Baritone;
        Sam Hartley, Entertainer and Compere;
        G. Stell Sugden at the Piano.
        ADMISSION TO SEATS - 3d. per person.
     Collection in aid of the Mayor's War Emergency Fund.

Thursday, 6th July:
  At the Open Air Swimming Pool, Marsden Park—at 2-0 p.m. (If wet, at the Public Baths, Bradley Road):
  CHILDREN'S SWIMMING GALA;
  POLO MATCH, between N.F.S. Teams.

In Victoria Park at 7-30 p.m. (If wet, in the Weavers' Institute):
  THE SAVOY CONCERT PARTY—
  Anne Makinson, Soprano;   Tom Hartley, Tenor;
  Dora Blaney, Contralto;   William Taylor, Baritone;
  Parker Chadwick, Comedian;   Jack Haworth, at the Piano.
        ADMISSION TO SEATS - 3d. per person.
     Collection in aid of the Mayor's War Emergency Fund.

Saturday, 8th July:
On the Public Bowling Greens:
  BOWLING FINALS.

Sunday, 9th July:
In Victoria Park—at 3 p.m. and 7-30 p.m.:
  THE HOME GUARD BAND "E" (Nelson) Company (28th Battalion).
        Conductor - CECIL H. BATESON.
        ADMISSION TO SEATS - 3d. per person.
     Collection in aid of the Home Guard Band Fund.

For fuller particulars of the daily events, watch the Board which will be placed in front of the Public Market (in Market Street).

                                F. W. ROBERTS,
Town Hall, Nelson.   Town Clerk.
  23rd June, 1944.

A SERIES OF

harvest. As it was many of the Leeds Road section had to make the journey on foot, and there was so much struggling on the return that many walked home. The gate was £137 – £20 more than the previous record, and judging by the cheers there appeared to be as many Nelsonians present as Colunians. Nelson achieved a decisive victory, but as it was only accomplished about 11 minutes from time, excitement was kept up until the last.[45]

Such occasions were common in towns like Nelson before and after the Second World War. It was only when other forms of entertainment, less local in their appeal and content, began to appear in the 'affluent' 1950s that local sport lost its power to embody the community in this way.

8

After 1945:
The Remaking of a Borough

North-East Lancashire contains the greatest cotton-weaving concentration in the world. It faces a re-development problem of considerable magnitude.[1]

For Nelson, as for many other northern industrial communities, the years after the Second World War presented enormous problems of change and adjustment in economic, social and political life. In some ways these years were as revolutionary in their impact as the late nineteenth century, which had seen the transformation of Marsden into Nelson. Unlike that period, however, local initiative counted for less in the post-1945 era. Whilst dynamic native entrepreneurship had been a critical factor in the making of Nelson, external influences played the crucial part in the remaking of the borough. Nelson's history in the second half of the twentieth century was made in the context of the international economic forces that the town and its people had shaped in the earlier years of the century. In this context local people and even national governments exercised only a limited influence. It could be argued, therefore, that this lack of power to control events has resulted in an incomplete readjustment of Nelson's economy and society.

Of Nelson, as of Britain generally, it might be said that, from the 1950s onwards, it lost an industry and failed to find a role. The 1930s had revealed serious structural problems for all sections of the Lancashire cotton industry, even for those firms producing the relatively high-quality cloths woven in Nelson. The switch into rayon had been significant in Nelson before 1939, indicating a willingness to move in the right direction towards a reconstituted industry. However, the war itself and the short-term boom that followed it had served to retard the impulse for radical change. The effects of state planning during the war, through the Cotton Control Board, might indeed have produced a feeling in some quarters that the industry could pull itself around. For example, John Williams, the managing director of Walter Pollard's Malvern Mills of Nelson, a man of vision who sought to encourage a co-operative spirit between employers and labour, sounded an optimistic note for the industry when addressing the Burnley Textile

Society at the end of 1945: 'Given a square deal [and] all-round co-operation to the fullest extent, Lancashire will rise again ...'.[2] Sir Amos Nelson had been similarly optimistic. His firm engaged in extensive rebuilding and modernisation at Valley Mills in the immediate post-war period, including the opening of a new weaving shed in 1947 with over 1,200 crêpe looms. At the time of his death in 1947, Amos Nelson was moving closer to the establishment of a weaving plant in Tasmania and was expressing very optimistic views about the future of his own firm and the industry at large.[3]

Such thinking was given credibility in the good trade of the late 1940s. Thanks to a plentiful stockpile of raw cotton at the end of the war, which cushioned Lancashire against price fluctuations, together with the need for overseas (especially Far Eastern) buyers to look to Lancashire for their cotton goods after the depredations of war, textile mills enjoyed something of a boom. But beneath this surface appearance of prosperity, problems remained. For one thing, the industry was having difficulties in attracting labour. The war itself was a cause of this, prompting the relocation of other industries to the North West out of the range of aerial bombing. By the end of the war, there was more alternative employment available than there had been in the past. With memories of the 1930s strong, many workers, especially the younger ones, preferred to put their faith in the alternatives to cotton. By 1948 the resultant issue of labour shortage was being confronted by the 'Cotton Campaign', which sought to encourage workers back to the mills, though with only limited success. The labour force in cotton was becoming a middle-aged one, less easy to redeploy when jobs became scarce. Robson, in his 1957 study of the cotton industry,[4] placed considerable emphasis on the fact that the industry was unable to take opportunities to re-establish itself in overseas markets in the immediate postwar years because of its inability to renew its depleted labour force. Pakistan, for example, engaged in a rapid industrialisation of cotton spinning at this time, supplying its own needs instead of turning to Lancashire. Another long-term problem was the uncertainty of Lancashire's export markets. As one perceptive observer had noted in the immediate aftermath of the war, overseas markets would 'in due course be served by others'[5] once defeated countries like Germany and Japan recovered. What was not foreseen, however, was a further problem – the challenge to be posed by overseas producers to Lancashire's domestic market. This was a problem that particularly affected Nelson, a town whose economy had to some extent been shielded from previous difficulties in a way that the economies of Blackburn and Burnley had not. By the 1950s, the combination of all these factors was producing a decline in the Lancashire cotton industry at the very time when, as Alan and Lesley Fowler have noted, the rest of the British economy was enjoying a period of relative 'affluence'.[6]

For Nelson, the decline was relatively sudden. It climaxed in the Cotton Industry Act of 1959. 'HERE LIES THE BODY OF KING COTTON', exclaimed the Labour *Nelson Gazette* on the eve of the 1959 general election, adding: 'recently deceased under Tory law.'[7] There was indeed a marked chronological correspondence between the presence in government of the Conservatives (1951–64) and the rapid decline of cotton, but whether the industry's problems can be ascribed so neatly to party political causes is less certain.

In spite of the coincidence of Labour governments and the period of boom in the late 1940s, it should be noted that neither the Labour nor the Conservative Party had produced much in the way of strategic thinking on the future of the cotton industry. A report by the Board of Trade in 1945, proposing a major reorganisation of the industry, had been largely ignored by both government and employers. Order books were filled by maintaining traditional methods and technology. Little innovation, especially of the automatic loom, was experienced. After 1951, in a period of decolonisation that had been inaugurated by Labour in the late 1940s, the Conservatives operated a free-trade policy which benefited Third World cotton manufacturers, especially those from the Commonwealth, enabling them to gain a toe-hold in the British market. At local level, by contrast, the idea of protecting Lancashire whilst simultaneously re-equipping the mills was being canvassed. Nelson weavers were active in demanding a more far-sighted vision from Westminster on these matters. In 1956 a delegation travelled to London to put the case to MPs for the introduction of a number of measures – more state aid for cotton, a restriction on the importing of cheap cotton goods, a re-examination of the trading relationships within the Commonwealth and a removal of purchase tax.[8]

The Cotton Industry Act of 1959 was in part a response to this kind of pressure. It was, though, premised upon two assumptions: first – in deference to Commonwealth producers – that protection was not acceptable; and, second, that contraction and reorganisation would make the industry more competitive 'in the markets of the world with the types of cloth that are wanted wherever living standards are high'.[9] The implementation of the Act involved a two-pronged approach. In the first place, the government would provided two-thirds of the costs of scrapping surplus machinery. However, redundancy payments to workers who lost their jobs as a consequence of this were not met by the state, but were made a charge upon the relevant sections of the industry. Secondly, on the recommendation of the Cotton Board, grants would be made available by the Board of Trade for re-equipping mills with more up-to-date machinery. To be eligible for such grants existing machinery had to have been scrapped by March 1960.

The Act provoked a ready response from employers in Nelson. This was received with dismay by the *Nelson Gazette*, which blamed the

ensuing closures not on the state of trade at the time, but on the
government's decision to contract the cotton industry. As one famous
name after another shut down over the next three years, the *Gazette*
felt moved to compare the attitude of present-day employers with that
of their predecessors in the 1930s, who 'hung on when times were
grim'.[10] There was some point in this remark. Conditions in Nelson
in the 1950s had scarcely been 'grim'. The town's industry had held

8.1 Marching to keep the cotton industry alive in 1962. A north-east Lancashire delegation takes possession of Oxford Street, London, in the aftermath of the Cotton
Industry Act of 1959, which sought to 'modernise' the industry, but threatened to de-
stroy it. In the front rank of the march are (from left to right) Sydney Silverman, the
berobed mayors of Nelson and Burnley, and Dan Jones (MP for Burnley). (*Lancashire
Library, Nelson Local Studies Collection*)

up reasonably well by comparison with other weaving centres. In the middle of the decade, for example, the labour force in weaving was still some 10,000 strong, compared with 12,000 at the outbreak of war in 1939. Only Burnley, by this time, had more people employed in weaving.[11] Nonetheless, 18 firms, with James Nelson's to the fore, immediately joined the 1959 scheme. Some 7,000 looms and 2,500 workers were thus identified as surplus to requirements. In all, the number of looms in Nelson had been halved by 1964 (10,000 from 22,000) and the proportion of cotton workers in the labour force had been reduced to 46 per cent. In a remarkably short period of time, Nelson had ceased to be a cotton town pure and simple. There was a feeling among some sections of local opinion that the 1959 Act, far from inaugurating a new era of modernisation, had simply put Nelson and Lancashire under the hammer; that the breaking-up of looms was simply the prelude to the breaking-up of the town. Nelson, which had resisted decline more effectively than some of its neighbours, succumbed more rapidly than anywhere else in the early 1960s.

There was a great deal of resentment among local people that the compensation paid to businesses did not find its way into reinvestment for new plant. 'How they got away with it is a mystery', claimed one local man. 'And what did weavers get after maybe 30 years with a firm? Perhaps £60 redundancy.'[12] The Act failed to stimulate any significant re-equipping. By 1964, of the 22 firms that had participated in the scheme since 1959, only 3 had installed automatic looms, and then only some 800. Of the 2,000 automatic looms in the town at this time, 30 per cent had been installed before 1959. The legend grew, not without foundation, that the Act had served employers rather than their workers and their town. 'They pocketed the money, never modernised and destroyed the industry'; 'When it happened, the employers were running all the way to the bank ...'.[13] The Nelson Gazette had estimated that, whereas a loom was valued at £80, a weaver was worth only around £56.[14]

There were a number of other repercussions for the cotton industry and its community aside from its diminution. One was unemployment, running at some 5 per cent in 1960. By comparison with some of the other old industrial areas – Northern Ireland, lowland Scotland and the North-east being among the most prominent – this rate of unemployment was relatively slight. But it heralded a problem that was to prove persistent throughout the next four decades. Official figures vary in their method of presentation (more recently, the percentage rate of unemployment for individual towns has often been overlooked in favour of a regional rate) and it is difficult to be precise about the level experienced in Nelson, but it seems likely that the rate hovered between 2 and 5 per cent in the 1970s. In the early part of 1980 it was at the same level as it had been 20 years earlier – 5 per cent. In company with the national trend, however, local unemployment rose quite steeply during the 1980s. By the time that the census of 1981 was compiled, in the early months of that year, the general unemployment level in the borough of Pendle had risen to 10 per cent. But this figure masked the fact that in the younger age groups (people between the ages of 16 and 24), it had risen to some 15 per cent for both men and women. Moreover, the sample census of that year revealed another interesting pattern. Of those who were 'economically active' approximately 20 per cent were working outside the district of their usual residence, travelling to work mainly by car but also, in a significant minority of cases, by bus.[15]

Another effect of cotton's decline was the rapid demise of the traditional small weaving firm and the relationships that had developed within it. Even in a relatively large company like Nelson's, there had been a sense of community and shared interests. Bosses and workers had often been on convivial terms, despite labour disputes, and whole families had worked at the same mill. Nelson's sports club, built by Amos Nelson in the 1920s as a memorial to men killed in the First World War, drew in all ranks of people and was one of the town's foremost institutions. 'I worked with Jimmy Nelson's all my life, our kids did, my mother did. Thousands used to work there ... it were a good shop, were Jimmy's.'[16] As smaller firms went under, they were often bought up by large combines, a process that was particularly encouraged after 1964 by the new Labour government under Harold Wilson. Local employers were replaced by outsiders whose knowledge of the industry was sometimes questioned ('They didn't know a shuttle from a duck's foot', according to one trade-union official[17]). Nelson's was taken over by one of the principal combines, Courtaulds, in 1963. This accelerated the process that had begun in Nelson in the 1930s with the switch to rayon. Mills were increasingly converted to the production of artifical fibre. The combines wove fibres, but they were not really weaving firms in the old sense so much as international, vertically integrated producers, a form of business organisation that had been initiated by Nelson's themselves in the interwar years. The presence of such combines now made it impossible to draw the distinction that had always existed between cotton and the rest of the textile industry. As a result, Nelson lost the crucial badge of distinctiveness that it had developed as a weaving town. When Courtaulds began to close Jimmy Nelson's Valley Mills in the early 1980s, after a period of difficult labour relations, it seemed as if the town's connection with cotton had at last come to an end.

The *Nelson Gazette*, in its campaign against the Cotton Industry Act, had urged that public money, instead of being used for compensating employers, should be directed towards the development of new industries in Lancashire. In this respect, despite optimistic forecasts by the

Leader and the *Gazette's* own claim in late 1960 that the local economy was 'booming',[18] Nelson was less well placed than other districts to diversify and renew its industrial base. Compared with Blackburn, for example, where decline had set in earlier, Nelson was too distant geographically to benefit from any spin-offs from the engineering success of Preston and Leyland. In fact, its poor road communications (until the 1980s) made it even less attractive as a place in which to invest than Burnley, which took most of the new industry that penetrated north-east Lancashire in the 1950s and 1960s. Writing in the mid-1960s, Freeman, Rogers and Kinvig singled out Nelson as an exceptional case where losses in the mill economy had not been outweighed by new occupations.[19] Of 13 mills converted to new purposes during the 1950s and early 1960s, only 4 employed more workers in 1962 than they had done in their previous use in 1951. There was also a feeling, frequently voiced by the business community since the 1930s, that Nelson's political reputation might have deterred prospective new businesses.

To counteract this, the Town Council, in the form of a Development Committee headed by Alderman Hoggarth and working closely with Sydney Silverman, lobbied vigorously to attract firms to Nelson. Great satisfaction was expressed in 1958, when Hygrade Corrugated Cases agreed to set up at Edward Street mill, and it was noted that the 'political outlook' of the town had not acted as a barrier to this important development.[20] But in spite of general optimism about the prospects for change in the early 1960s, progress was slow compared with other areas, and the government's decision in 1960 not to include north-east Lancashire on the list of areas qualifying for state assistance did not help matters. The district retained a higher proportion of cotton workers than many neighbouring areas, therefore, and the essentially Victorian economy survived longer here than elsewhere.

With the failure of government to offer any direct help to attract new industry, the optimism of the late 1950s gave way to a growing sense of crisis. In the spring of 1962 Nelson Town Council set up a Textile Action Committee; a petition launched by civic leaders in May of that year to 'Save the Lancashire Textile Industry' quickly accumulated 10,000 signatures. The Town Council, in conjunction with the North-east Lancashire Development Committee and the Lancashire and Merseyside Industrial Development Association, was active in publicising the benefits of Nelson. But the prospect of cheap land and housing, good services and up-to-date technical education produced no dramatic response from the business community, and there was no speedy transformation in the local economy. Change came slowly. In 1964, for example, a Corporation guide that was designed to present Nelson in its most appealing light was able to list relatively few new business developments: glass fibre moulding at Hendon Mill,

pie-making at Lonsdale Bakery (dating from 1957), the manufacture of
wrapping and packaging machines at the Vulcan Works, and the wall-
paper company Coloroll, which arrived with 300 jobs in 1964, were
some of the more prominent recent ventures. Many old names, however,
were still present – Coulton's printers and stationers, Duckworth's mills
at Reedyford and Pendle Street, Fells cloths, Fryer's 'Victory V' con-
fectionery, and Hill's pharmaceuticals at Spring Bank Works, a
wholesale chemists which had been supplying local hospitals since 1954,

8.2 New industry on old sites. Three examples of the conversion of old premises to new uses. At Seedhill Mills (opposite, top), built in the 1870s, the firm of J. R. Battye spins wool for use in the making of carpets. Ecroyd's industrial colony at Lomeshaye (opposite, bottom) has become the site for new premises housing a variety of modern manufacturing and processing companies. At the White Walls Industrial Estate (above), on the Nelson–Colne border, a similar range of businesses has been established, as well as a retail park including a supermarket and a mill store which attracts shoppers from across the region.

after trading as a retail chemists since the early years of the century. There was scarcely concealed disappointment that Nelson had attracted little engineering, unlike Burnley, which had been a base for Lucas's since the war, or Blackburn, where Mullard's had set up in 1954.

Changes had gradually occurred some 30 years later, in no small measure because of the improvements to road communications in the 1980s. A Pendle motorway link – anticipated by the *Leader* in 1968 as the area's 'lifeline'[21] – finally came in 1983. It was accompanied by the designation of the Lomeshaye and the White Walls industrial estates as enterprise zones, giving 100 per cent allowances against income tax and freedom from business rates for 10 years. Three other industrial concentrations also developed in the town, attracting a variety of businesses. They ranged from the Peter Reed Group, a family business manufacturing high-quality bed linen at Lomeshaye – where in 1986 they opened the first weaving shed to be built in Nelson for over 60 years – to P.H.S. Nelson Ltd, which handles major promotions for national newspapers and consumer-goods manufacturers using a Nelson PO box number. Another development to reflect the decline of cotton production was the opening of retail outlets in the premises of former mills. Throughout Lancashire, the 'factory shop' phenomemon had become a notable contribution to the shopping and leisure boom of the 1980s, with old industrial buildings earning their keep by attracting bargain hunters from a wide area. In some cases, such as Carrington-Viyella, in Sam Holden's old Holmefield Mill at Barrowford, or the East Lancashire Towel Company, also at Barrowford, textile products are retailed direct to the public from working mills. In others – the Boundary Mill stores on the White Walls industrial estate on the Nelson–Colne border being a case in point – an old weaving mill houses a range of departments offering consumer goods including shoes, ladies and men's wear, and home furnishings. The store even provides a 'men's lounge', with 'comfortable chairs, satellite sport TV, newspapers and magazines'. Gender divisions are reproduced even in the world of modern shopping. By the summer of 1994, some 355 companies were trading in the borough of Pendle in a variety of business classifications.

Table 8.1. Businesses in Pendle, mid-1990s

Type of activity	No. of Companies	% of total
Chemicals	24	6.7
Construction	43	12.1
Metals	73	20.5
Electrical/electronic engineering	23	6.5
Vehicles, etc.	16	4.5
Food and drink	13	3.7
Textiles/clothing/footwear	46	12.9
Timber/wooden furniture	23	6.5
Paper/printing	24	6.7
Transport/communications	9	2.5
Miscellaneous industrial and commercial services	61	17.1
TOTAL	355	

(*Source*: Borough of Pendle, *Companies Register*, Nelson, 1994)

The district has thus gradually acquired a more diversified economy in which textiles and related products, though continuing to be a significant sector, are not the most important source of labour. The change was symbolised in the residency of Valley Mills, once the home of James Nelson's company. After Courtaulds had removed, the premises housed a series of engineering firms in the early 1990s, including Fort Vale Engineering Ltd, a leading producer of container tank fittings using advanced computer-controlled equipment. The firm twice won the Queen's Award for Export Achievement during the 1980s. More to the point, perhaps, is the fact that the main centre of Valley Mills – the two weaving sheds – were demolished in the early 1990s. The new economic base, moreover, possesses an exaggerated form of an old pattern of industrial organisation. Large firms, such as Rolls-Royce at Barnoldswick and Smith and Nephew at Colne, Brier-field and Nelson, which employ over 1,000 people each, are rare. The predominant unit is the small business, whose virtues were so keenly extolled in Conservative Party circles in the 1980s – firms with between one and 24 employees. Two-thirds of all companies in Pendle in 1994 were of this type, with over 30 per cent of all firms having fewer than ten employees. The conditions for trade-unionism in these circumstances are not propitious, and thus another notable trend in the local economy has been reversed, exemplified by the closure of the office of the Nelson Weavers' Association in 1991. Whether initiatives of this type have provided the district with its economic renaissance remains to be seen. Firms of this size are not always the most stable and, where they constitute a high proportion of the economic activity of a district, it can mean frequent turnover of business and a degree of uncertainty in employment prospects. In fact, unemployment became a persistent problem of local economic life during the 1960s and continues to be so.[22] As in so many other cases of 'new town' development and 'enterprise' activity, it is by no means certain that those ventures attracted by the various fiscal inducements of national government will be able to stay when the economic going gets tough. As far as the future is concerned, north-east Lancashire faces a problem that is likely to affect other parts of the North – that of 'peripherality'. With a growing concentration of economic wealth and activity in the south-east of England, and an increasing tendency – as a result of communications links such as the Channel Tunnel and the railways that serve it – for this area to look towards the European continent, there is a danger of the North becoming marginalised. Fear of this has led to the promotion of the 'Trans-Pennine' theme among northern-based businessmen and economists – the idea of an economic corridor running from the Mersey and Ribble to the Humber, alongside the M62 motorway, using the Humber ports as access to the single market of the EU. Were this to come about, it could offer a lifeline to the Nelson area.[23]

One aspect of the attempted reorganisation of the cotton industry after 1959 produced the most significant social change to affect Nelson in recent times: immigration. This resulted from both long- and short-term factors. In the long term, Nelson, in common with many other Lancashire textile towns, had been experiencing a steady loss of population since the 1930s. The 1931 population of 38,300 had declined to 34,400 by 1951 and 32,300 ten years later. By the time of the 1966 sample census, it was 31,800; 31,250 by 1971. Migration accounted for

most of this population loss, which was helpful in the sense that it served
to moderate the unemployment levels caused by the decline of the
cotton industry. In another sense, however, it proved to be a drawback.
The migrants tended to be younger people, leaving the average age of
the remaining population relatively high. This in turn affected both the
birth and death rates, as the age structure of the population was skewed
towards the less fertile, more elderly age groups, a situation which only
began to right itself during the course of the 1970s (see Table 8.2).

**Table 8.2. Age structure of population in Nelson (1971) and
            Pendle (1981) (%)**

Age group	1971	1981
0–4	7.6	6.8 [6.0]
5–15	15.2	16.0 [16.3]
16–24	13.9	13.2 [14.1]
25–44	21.4	25.1 [26.3]
45–65	20.7*	19.0 [19.7]
65 +	24.4	20.0 [17.7]

Notes: Figures in square brackets = national %s.
* average of men and women.

Source: *Census of England and Wales, 1971, 1981* (HMSO,
London).

Nelson therefore had a preponderance of middle-aged people in its
labour force, perhaps less receptive to new ideas, at a time when attempts
were being made to revitalise its industry. These attempts involved, in
the short term, a series of innovations in working practices, principally
revolving around the introduction of shiftworking. To be utilised economically, new machinery required double- and triple-shift operation.
Being unaccustomed to this method of working, Lancashire operatives
were generally resistant to it. Except for the short 'housewives' shift'
in the evening, female workers were particularly hostile because of its
impact on the domestic routine. Coupled with this was an opposition
to travelling to relocated places of work. Unable to recruit school-
leavers, and experiencing a loss of older workers either through
retirement or the counter-attractions of other work, employers turned
their attention to a new source of labour from overseas.

8.3 Innovation and adaptation by new Nelsonians. Nelson's second wave of immigration occurred almost 100 years after the first, with the arrival in the 1960s of Punjabi workers and their families from Pakistan. Their newly built places of worship contrast sharply with the Lancashire landscape and Victorian domestic architecture. Some properties have been converted to new uses, such as this advice centre in Cross Street. The Sunni Moslem community is a vibrant one, with a variety of welfare, youth and sporting organisations.

When faced with a labour shortage in the 1940s, cotton employers had often sought to recruit employees from the European Volunteer Workers – people (often women) from countries such as Poland, the Ukraine and Czechoslovakia who had been rendered homeless by

the war. In the 1960s the solution was sought in the recruitment of
Asian labour. Mill officials made recruitment tours of villages in the
Indian sub-continent offering free passage and good wages: according
to one sceptical Nelson weaver, they 'offered them Eldorado if they
came to Lancashire'.[24] The policy proved successful, at least as far as
ensuring a labour supply was concerned. Shift-working, especially night-
shifts, was made possible by immigrant workers, who in Nelson came
mainly from Pakistan – to be precise, from villages in the Gujarat
district of the Punjab. In the early 1960s the migrants were almost
exclusively male, as is often the case in such situations. Families followed
on a few years later, when it became apparent that the original hope
of returning to Pakistan ('the myth of return', as sociologists have
termed it) was not likely to be realised. By the time the census of 1981
was compiled the new administrative area of Pendle (including Nelson,
Colne, Brierfield and Barnoldswick as its main centres of population)
contained over 5,000 persons living in houses where the head of the
household had been born in Pakistan. This was almost 90 per cent of
all the New Commonwealth residents in the borough. Of these, over
2,000 (41 per cent) had been born in the United Kingdom, 97 per cent
of them being 15 years old or less, born since the mid-1960s; 58 per
cent had been born outside the UK, and two-thirds of these were
between the ages of 16 and 44. It was, therefore, a relatively young
population, especially compared to all those born in the UK (and where
the head of the household was born in the UK) of whom only 38 per
cent were between the ages of 16 and 44, and 40 per cent were over
the age of 45.

In the town that had lionised Learie Constantine, the arrival of Asian
workers en masse presented problems in the 1960s. How quickly and
to what extent the old radical culture of Nelson was able to transform
itself into a multicultural community is a problematical question. For
indigenous workers, in spite of traditions of trade-union solidarity and
mill camaraderie, there has been a tendency to see Pakistani immigrants
as responsible for the plight of the white working class. A comment
made to Priscilla Ross in her study of Nelson – 'I'm not racialist, but
it's not fair the way it's gone. We've slogged ourselves to death for
what? Now we can't sell our houses here … All the slogging seems to
have been a waste of time'[25] – sums up what must have been a fairly
general mood. This is reflected to a certain extent in local newspapers,
the contents of which, in the 1960s and 1970s, gave little sense of the
new ethnic composition of the borough. What is striking is what is not
said about immigrants rather than what is.[26]

Early immigrants were usually single males, working almost exclusively on the night shift in Nelson mills. Their hoped-for promotion
rarely materialised. 'We hoped to go on and do something else, train
perhaps, but most of us have stayed as workers working the nights.'[27]

8.4 Spectators at Seedhill cricket ground, c. 1950, clothed for a fickle climate. An ageing breed? The club had been a focus of town loyalty and had drawn support from a wide range of people. Large crowds of 10,000 and more attended matches in the 1930s, though by the late 1950s spectating was in decline as alternative attractions beckoned. (*Lancashire Library, Nelson Local Studies Collection*)

The rise in unemployment in the 1980s hit this generation of immigrant workers especially hard, with the result that prospects for the 50+ age group are extremely limited. Lacking skills, educational qualifications and even, in some cases, English-language abilities, the likelihood of long-term unemployment for this group is great. Their children, born in the area, are better-placed. Having gone through the educational system (including universities in some cases), their transferable skills are greater and their expectations higher. As one commentator has noted of this group: 'low status, low pay and manual jobs are no longer the *only* options as they were for the parent generation'.[28]

Asian workers have nevertheless built their own community and institutions. By the 1980s a range of very active cultural organisations had been developed in Nelson and Brierfield. It included – in addition to mosques, schools, advice and welfare centres – a society for Asian disabled and a centre for ethnic elderly people. The latter was unique in Lancashire. For younger people the Pendle and District Cricket League had exclusively Asian teams by the 1990s. Altogether 19 separate cultural Asian and Muslim organisations were listed in a survey conducted in the later 1980s, testimony to a vibrant community.[29] By contrast, this period saw the decline of many of the associations and institutions from which a sense of community had previously been cultivated among the indigenous population. The chapels continued the decline that had set in during the interwar years, in many cases selling off their buildings for other purposes. Mill closures meant a loss of the sense of workplace identity, including works sports teams. A similar picture was evident in the bigger sports clubs. Though the standard of cricket remained good in the Lancashire League, there was

a marked falling away in spectator support during the 1960s, and only
very rarely were the packed grounds which had been so common in
the 1930s to be witnessed thereafter. Club treasurers, always worried
about the effects of bad weather on spectator levels, now became
reconciled to searching for a permanent alternative to gate receipts as
the basis for club finances. They found them in bar-takings, fruit
machines and soccer pools. Above all, perhaps, the sense of lost identity
for Nelsonians came with the local government reform of the early
1970s. Nelson ceased to exist as an independent borough in 1974 and
was integrated in a new borough, Pendle.

In writing about the years after the Second World War, many
historians have been accustomed to speak of 'affluence'. Full employment, the development of the welfare state and the rise of consumerism
have been seen as the essential hallmarks of this economic and social
trend, expressed in the course of the general election campaign of 1959
as 'you've never had it so good'. Though some caution is needed when
applying the term, it does nevertheless seem a valid way of thinking
about material experiences in Britain in the 1950s and 1960s. Whether
it has much relevance for a town like Nelson, however, is another
matter. This period of alleged affluence coincided with the most critical
shift in the foundations of Nelson's economy for a hundred years. For
many, the late 1950s and early 1960s were a time of anxiety and
uncertainty. A number of measures of affluence might be examined in
this context. The main one – jobs – was, as we have already seen,
problematical. Another is housing. By the early 1970s, some 70 per
cent of all households in Nelson were owned by the people who lived
in them. But this was not in itself a product of the postwar boom. The
district had exhibited this pattern historically: most people bought,
rather than rented, their homes. By the 1960s, however, much of
Nelson's housing stock was old. With the exception of municipal
initiatives there had been little new building. In the early 1970s over
25 per cent of households still had no inside toilet, and only two-thirds
of all properties had exclusive use of hot water, a fixed bath and an
internal wc, a statistic which revealed scarcely any improvement since
1961. This pattern was not uncommon in the region generally. As a
report commissioned by the Department of the Environment in 1971
commented:

> the sub-region [North-East Lancashire] is now faced with the classic
> problems of Victorian 'boom' areas: loss of employment and popu-
> lation, low incomes and slow growth of services, areas of derelict and
> near-derelict land, obsolete housing and industrial premises; and the
> resulting low level of its local authorities' rate income limits their
> capacity to tackle these problems.[30]

A further index of affluence, perhaps the most noticeable, was car ownership. During the 1970s the number of households in Lancashire with no car available for use fell from 50 per cent to 40 per cent. These figures are revealing in themselves. In Pendle – an area in which mobility in search of work was important – 45 per cent of households still had no access to a car in 1981. The regional figure was 41 per cent, the national was 39 per cent; 42.9 per cent possessed a car and only 11.6 per cent had two or more cars (the national figure being 15.5 per cent).[31] The case of Nelson should remind us, therefore, to approach the idea of 'affluence' with a certain amount of circumspection when using it to describe the changes of the postwar period.

The social and cultural changes of these years are matched by political ones. In their way, these have been equally dramatic. The decline of cotton and the arrival of immigrants were gradual processes. Political change was signalled above all by a single momentous event: the 1968 by-election in the Nelson and Colne constituency, occasioned by the death of Sydney Silverman, when over 30 years of Labour representation were overturned and the seat became Conservative with a majority of 3,522.

As with all political changes there were long-term causes at work. The constituency of Nelson and Colne, though held continuously by Labour since 1935, had always been marginal in character, especially after 1945. The Conservatives had usually polled a respectable proportion of the vote, and although Nelson itself was solid for Labour, this loyalty was not replicated in other parts of the constituency. Moreover, the social character of some districts changed gradually as areas like Barrowford and Reedly acquired a new middle-class population. The old socialist culture of Nelson itself was also losing some of its liveliness. With economic changes, long-established institutions disappeared. The Co-op was facing a difficult future as a retail organisation by the early 1960s, the *Nelson Gazette* ceased publication in the summer of 1962, and, with the shrinkage of its membership, the costs of maintaining the Weavers' Institute were becoming too high. But, for all that, the change of 1968 was abrupt, its suddenness emphasised by the fact that, in the general election two years earlier, Sydney Silverman had secured a comfortable majority, in spite of the campaign having been clouded by the 'Moors Murders' and the issue of capital punishment, of which Silverman had long been the principal opponent. Silverman's death, however, removed a long and honourable connection with Labour and a strong personal vote, which their new candidate, Betty Boothroyd, could not command, especially in the economic circumstances of the late 1960s. For what seems to have been the chief factor in the result was the failure of the Labour government to arrest the decline of cotton. The irony of this was that, in opposition, the Prime Minister, Harold Wilson, had been the foremost Labour politician to confront the problems of the industry. By 1968, however, disenchantment with Labour was deeply ingrained in the constituency. Though party activists took some comfort in the fact that the result – representing a swing of 11.4 per cent to the Conservatives – was much less than in other by-elections at the time, there was little doubt that it was apathy on the part of the formerly radical textile workers, then still comprising 40 per cent of the labour force, that sealed Labour's fate. 'Even if Miss Boothroyd had been handing out gold-plated guarantees of lower taxes', claimed Joseph Minogue in *The Guardian*, 'it is doubtful whether [people] would have been impressed.'[32] The Conservatives were also helped by two other factors. Firstly, their candidate, David Waddington, was a local man from Sabden who had fought the seat in 1964. More important was the fact that over 4,000 votes were taken up by a Liberal (the first in the constituency since 1929) and a nationalist candidate, Brian Tattersall, who polled over 1,200 votes campaigning to repatriate immigrant workers who were, he alleged, 'disillusioned and unhappy' and wanted to go 'home'.[33]

The link with Labour was not completely broken. For one thing, in April 1968 the Weavers' Institute was transformed into a social and cultural centre named Silverman Hall. In this symbolic form, a famous name from the past lived on. So, too, in local politics, did Nelson's commitment to Labour. The local government reorganisation of 1974 deprived Nelson of the powers that it had won in 1890, as the former borough was subsumed in the new borough of Pendle. Nelson's 8 wards were merged into the new 19 of Pendle, which included a number of areas where support for Labour had never been much in evidence. This worked to the advantage of the Liberal Party, which, by the 1990s, controlled the Council Chamber with strength based in Colne and Barnoldswick. It was very noticeable, however, that Nelson's attachment to Labour was as firm as it had always been. In 1995, of the 18 councillors elected in Nelson's 6 wards, all but 2 were Labour; the others were Liberal. Moreover, Labour's strongest wards in Nelson are often those, like Walverden, where the Asian immigrants and their children make up the majority of the electorate. The town therefore remains inhospitable territory for Conservatism. In parliamentary elections, the 1970s saw Nelson and Colne swing between the two major parties, but in the landmark election of 1979 it was captured for the Conservatives by John Lee. He held the seat throughout the 1980s, when it ceased to be Nelson and Colne and became the new constituency of Pendle, its boundaries coterminous with those of the borough. In 1992 Labour reclaimed its parliamentary inheritance when Gordon Prentice took the Pendle seat with a swing of 4.5 per cent in a turnout of 83 per cent. The constituency had always had a high level of owner-occupiers (75 per cent in 1981, rising to 79 per cent in 1991). Many of them lived in small terraced houses, and a major cause of

8.5 The construction of the Arndale Centre, 1967 (top). This is the same spot from which the photograph on p. 17 was taken over 60 years earlier. With this central area redevelopment, Nelson gained a shopping centre, but perhaps lost some of its soul. The collection of buildings that had been the town centre since the late nineteenth century might not have been distinguished, but they were unique. Arndale Centres seemed to spring up everywhere in the 1960s and 1970s. Nevertheless, the pedestrian area and gardens (bottom) can provide an atmosphere of unhurried calm on occasions, even if the architecture is not compelling. (*Lancashire Library, Nelson Local Studies Collection*)

disillusionment with the Conservatives was the establishment of the poll tax, which had increased the burdens on these small house owners, who had previously paid comparatively low rates.[34]

The election of the left-winger Gordon Prentice as MP forms one link with the past alongside many changes in contemporary Nelson. Perhaps the most surprising of these – certainly to anyone returning to the town after several years' absence – is the ease with which it is now possible to miss Nelson altogether. In contrast with the tortuous road journey of former times, the M65 can now take the unwary motorist straight past the town in the blinking of an eye. Once in the town, Nelson presents the visitor with a rather uneasy juxtaposition of the old and the new. Some parts – the southerly end of Carr Road approaching the town centre, for example, still dominated by the Methodist Chapel and solid Victorian villas long since converted to offices – seem little changed since the early years of the century. By comparison, the redeveloped central area, with its Arndale Centre and pedestrian ways, has an architecture inspired by the styles of the 1960s and American notions of concentrated retail centres. It is fashionable nowadays to deride such developments without noting their advantages. In Nelson, the opening of the first phase of the Arndale Centre in 1968 improved the town centre from the point of view of the shopper, providing a completely enclosed precinct of attractive shops and market stalls which subsequently became the focus of a pedestrianised central area. The hazards involved in crossing the busy meeting point of five main roads were removed, creating a town centre for people rather than cars – 'a shopper's dream', according to a recent publicity brochure. However, the Arndale development is virtually an island in both style and place. For one thing, what was once a collection of undistinguished though integrated town-centre buildings – because they were all constructed at more or less the same time – has become a mixture reflecting different conceptions of urban development. Moreover, in order to accommodate the motor car, an inner ring-road system has been built for through traffic which seals off the shopping centre from the southerly parts of the town. Where once the routes from this direction converged naturally at the centre, the inner ring road now seems to act as a barrier.

Nelson was never an attractive town; even in its official publicity, it was the town's practical attributes that were emphasised. Its buildings were not of conventional architectural merit. In fact, it had few built features of any kind that might have tempted visitors for aesthetic reasons. The architectural historian Nikolaus Pevsner, whose ideas of good architecture were essentially to do with churches and stately homes, was very disparaging about the town: 'Nelson has no past and no architectural shape ... Only the parish church keeps up a civic dignity'.[35] As Pevsner recognised, its chief virtue visually is the natural landscape surrounding the town. This now plays its part in the attempt to revive the region economically through tourism. The countryside is made use of for walks, picnic sites and ramblers' routes. In the recreation of the district for tourist purposes, it is the pre-industrial past that is celebrated; in, for example, the Pendle Heritage Centre at Barrowford, based upon the Bannisters' fine old house at Park Hill, mainly seventeenth-century with some eighteenth-century embellishments; and in those villages in the shadow of Pendle Hill, whose population once provided Nelson's labour force ('picturesque villages straddle along the borough, each endowed with something to enchant the visitor', as the publicity brochure describes them). In Nelson itself this process is typified by the development of Walverden Reservoir as a recreation area offering fishing, bird-watching and quiet walks. Whether this process of transforming the district into one of physical attractions can go much further is doubtful. There is probably still too much evidence of industrial decay in a town like Nelson for it to have commercial potential as a 'beautified' northern urban landscape, tempting the middle classes to buy up and modernise cheap property. By comparison with older market towns like Clitheroe and even Colne, Nelson possesses few charms.

The town built around the crossroads now faces a metaphorical crossroads as far as its future is concerned. When the authors of the Lancashire county plan spoke, in 1950, of the 'redevelopment problem of considerable magnitude' that faced the region, they can scarcely have imagined the nature of the task facing a town like Nelson. The following year, the town's largest employer, James Nelson, published a commemorative history of the firm which could both look back on a successful past and, what is more to the point, anticipate a rosy future. Though there were economic problems of some severity in the 1950s, Nelson had not changed radically from what it was like at the turn of the century. It was the sudden change of the 1960s, in the aftermath of the Cotton Industry Act, that brought the problems of redevelopment starkly into focus. Whether the nineteenth-century new town has succeeded in confronting these problems and remaking itself, with a viable economic base as part of a new borough, is a question that remains to be answered in the twenty-first century.

Notes

Chapter 1

1. 'The Growth of Nelson and Brierfield', *Preston Guardian*, 12 February 1881.
2. John K. Walton, *Lancashire: A Social History 1558–1939* (Manchester University Press, Manchester: 1987), p. 219.
3. W. Bennett, *The History of Marsden and Nelson* (Nelson Corporation, Nelson: 1957).
4. Jill Liddington, *The Life and Times of a Respectable Rebel: Selina Cooper (1864–1946)* (Virago, London: 1984); Alan and Lesley Fowler, *The History of the Nelson Weavers' Association* (Burnley, Nelson, Rossendale and District Textile Workers' Union, Nelson: n.d.); Jane Mark-Lawson, 'Women, Welfare and Urban Politics: A Comparative Analysis of Luton and Nelson, 1917–1934' (Ph.D. thesis, Lancaster University, 1987); Priscilla Ross, 'A Town Like Nelson: the Social Implications of Technical Change in a Lancashire Mill Town' (D.Phil. thesis, Sussex University, 1991).
5. See Eric E. Lampard, 'The Urbanizing World', in H. J. Dyos and Michael Wolff (eds), *The Victorian City: Images and Realities*, vol. 2 (Routledge and Kegan Paul, London: 1973), pp. 3–58; Pierre Merlin, *New Towns: Regional Planning and Development* (Methuen, London: 1971).
6. David F. Crew, *Town in the Ruhr: a Social History of Bochum 1860–1914* (Columbia University Press, New York: 1979), pp. 7–10.
7. T. W. Freeman, H. B. Rogers and R. H. Kinvig, *Lancashire, Cheshire and the Isle of Man* (Nelson, London: 1966), p. 7.
8. See David James, *Bradford* (Ryburn Publishing, Halifax: 1990).
9. See Bennett, *Marsden and Nelson*, ch. 5; William Farrer and J. Brownbill (eds), *Victoria History of the County of Lancaster*, vol. 6 (University of London Institute of Historical Research, London: 1911, reprinted 1966), pp. 536–43.
10. See W. Bennett, *The History of Burnley* (Burnley Corporation, Burnley: 1951), ch. 1; Dorothy Harrison (ed.), *The History of Colne* (Pendle Heritage Centre, Barrowford: 1988), ch. 8.
11. Charles Hadfield, *British Canals: An Illustrated History* (David and Charles, Newton Abbot: 1979), pp. 86–9.
12. Geoffrey Timmins, *The Last Shift: The Decline of Handloom Weaving in Nineteenth Century Lancashire* (Manchester University Press, Manchester: 1993), pp. 184–6.
13. *Nelson Leader* (hereafter *NL*), 16 November 1906. See also M. E. W. Brooker, 'Nelson and Colne in the Industrial Revolution', B.A. dissertation (University of Cambridge, 1975), p. 32.
14. Philip Viscount Snowden, *An Autobiography: vol. 1, 1864–1919* (Ivor Nicholson and Watson, London: 1934), p. 40.
15. Liddington, *Respectable Rebel*, chs 1–4.
16. Nikolaus Pevsner, *The Buildings of England: Lancashire 2 – The Rural North* (Penguin Books, London: 1969), p. 180.

Chapter 2

1. *Nelson Chronicle* (hereafter *NC*), 18 April 1890.
2. D. A. Farnie, *The English Cotton Industry and the World Market 1815–96* (Clarendon Press, Oxford: 1979), p. 310.
3. W. Bennett, *The History of Marsden and Nelson* (Nelson Corporation, Nelson: 1957), p. 201.

4. Farnie, *English Cotton Industry*, pp. 284–5, 308, 310.
5. Alan and Lesley Fowler, *The History of the Nelson Weavers' Association* (Burnley, Nelson, Rossendale and District Textile Workers' Union, Nelson: n.d.), p. 3.
6. *Colne and Nelson Times* (hereafter *CNT*), 15, 22 September 1911.
7. Farnie, *English Cotton Industry*, p. 29.
8. *CNT*, 13 October 1911; Bennett, *Marsden and Nelson*, p. 197.
9. *Nelsons of Nelson: The Story of James Nelson Ltd, 1881–1951* (Harley Publishing Co., London: 1951); *NL*, 4 October 1912.
10. *CNT*, 3 November 1911.
11. *CNT*, 3 November 1911.
12. Farnie, *English Cotton Industry*, p. 310.
13. Joseph and Frank Nasmith, *Recent Cotton Mill Construction and Engineering* (John Heywood Ltd., Manchester: 1909), ch. 7.
14. Lars G. Sandberg, *Lancashire in Decline: a Study in Entrepreneurship, Technology, and International Trade* (Ohio State University Press, Columbus, Ohio: 1974). See also Mary B. Rose (ed.), *The Lancashire Cotton Industry: A History since 1700* (Lancashire County Books, Preston: 1996).
15. *Census of England and Wales, 1921* (London: 1922).
16. See Michael Savage, *The Dynamics of Working Class Politics: the Labour Movement in Preston 1880–1940* (Cambridge University Press, Cambridge: 1987).
17. S. J. Chapman, *Lancashire Cotton Industry: a Study in Economic Development* (Manchester University Press, Manchester: 1904), p. 160. The ratio was 100 (men) : 85 (women).
18. *Census of England and Wales, 1921*.
19. See George Henry Wood, *History of Wages in the Cotton Trade During the Past 100 Years* (Sherratt and Hughes, London: 1910), pp. 83–5; Fowler, *Nelson Weavers*, pp. 22–3.
20. *Supplement to the Annual Report of the Chief Inspector of Factories and Workshops 1900* (London: 1901).
21. *NL*, 27 March 1914.
22. *Census of England and Wales*, 1901; *NL*, 8 May 1914; Michael Winstanley (ed.), *Working Children in Nineteenth Century Lancashire* (Lancashire County Books, Preston: 1995).
23. Priscilla Ross, 'A Town like Nelson: The Social Implications of Technical Change in a Lancashire Mill Town' (D.Phil. thesis, Sussex University, 1991), pp. 56, 94, 98.
24. H. A. Turner, *Trade Union Growth, Structure and Policy: A Comparative Study of the Cotton Unions* (George Allen and Unwin, London: 1962), III, ch. 2.
25. See Jeffrey Hill, 'Working Class Politics in Lancashire, 1885–1906: A Study in the Regional Origins of the Labour Party' (Ph.D. thesis, University of Keele, 1969), ch. 2.
26. Janet Weinroth, *Little Moscow* (1976), p. 8. (24-pp. unpublished typescript in Nelson Public Library, based on notes made by Professor H. Weinroth, University of Montreal, for a comparative study of Nelson and Darwen. Professor Weinroth died before completing his work).
27. Fowler, *Nelson Weavers*, pp. 9–11.
28. Joseph L. White, *The Limits of Trade Union Militancy: The Lancashire Textile Workers 1910–14* (Greenwood Press, Westport, Conn.: 1978).
29. Details from White, *Trade Union Militancy*, pp. 142–73.
30. White, *Trade Union Militancy*, p. 169.
31. *NL*, 2 January 1914.
32. Fowler, *Nelson Weavers*, p. 23.
33. *NL*, 7 August, 9 October 1914.

Chapter 3

1. T. Chippendale, 'Welcome to the Charter', *Nelson Chronicle* (hereafter *NC*), 5 September 1890.
2. *NC*, 5 September 1890.
3. *Tithe Award for Great and Little Marsden, 1842* (Nelson Public Library, copied from

the original). I am grateful to Mrs S. Byrne, Nelson Local History Librarian, for drawing my attention to this source.

4. Janet Weinroth, *Little Moscow* (1976), p. 8.
5. *NL*, 17 April 1904, 19 October 1934; W. F. Ecroyd folder, Local History Collection; Henry Foulds, *A Selection of Newspaper Reports from Local Newspapers, 1875–80* (both at Nelson Public Library).
6. W. Bennett, *The History of Marsden and Nelson* (Nelson Corporation, Nelson: 1957), p. 175.
7. *NC*, 5 September 1890.
8. *NC*, 5 September 1890.
9. *NC*, 5 September 1890.
10. *CNT*, 9 June 1888.
11. *NC*, 5 September 1890.
12. *NC*, 11 April 1890.
13. Jill Liddington, *The Life and Times of a Respectable Rebel: Selina Cooper (1864–1946)* (Virago, London: 1984), p. 33.
14. See W. Bennett, *The History of Burnley* (Burnley Corporation, Burnley: 1951), iv, ch. 2; Chushichi Tsuzuki, *H. M. Hyndman and British Socialism* (Oxford University Press, London: 1961), p. 97.
15. Bennett, *Marsden and Nelson*, p. 209.
16. Weinroth, *Little Moscow*, p. 7.
17. See Lynn Hollen Lees, *Exiles of Erin: Irish Migrants in Victorian London* (Manchester University Press, Manchester: 1979); Daniel Lawrence, *Black Migrants: White Natives, A Study of Race Relations in Nottingham* (Cambridge University Press, Cambridge: 1974).
18. *Ebenezer: Being an Account of the Central Gospel Mission, Nelson 1890–1929* (Nelson: 1929) (Nelson Public Library).
19. James Vickers, *History of Independent Methodism* (Bolton: 1920); Joseph Robinson, *Salem: Independent Methodist Church, Nelson: A Short History 1852–1952* (Independent Methodist Church, Nelson: 1952) (Nelson Public Library).
20. Liddington, *Respectable Rebel*, pp. 37–8.
21. *St Mary the Virgin, Diamond Jubilee Celebrations March 25th/26th 1939, 1879–1939* (Nelson Public Library).
22. See *Almanac for the Diocese of Salford, 1900*; Liddington, *Respectable Rebel*, pp. 314–36; George I. Hawkes, *The Development of Public Education in Nelson* (Nelson Corporation, Nelson: 1966), chs 6 and 7.
23. John K. Walton, *Lancashire: A Social History 1558–1939* (Manchester University Press, Manchester: 1979), p. 299.
24. As in some other Lancashire towns: Bury, Preston, St Helens, Stockport and Wigan: *Elementary Education Returns 1900* (London: 1901).
25. Bennett, *Marsden and Nelson*, pp. 192–3; William Farrer and J. Brownbill (eds), *Victoria History of the County of Lancaster*, vol. 6 (University of London Institute of Historical Research, London: 1911, reprinted 1966), p. 542; Hawkes, *The Development of Public Education in Nelson*.
26. Nelson Co-operative and Industrial Society, *Jubilee Souvenir 1860–1910* (Co-operative Press, Manchester: 1910); *Co-operative Directory, 1887, 1896* (Central Co-operative Board, Manchester); Barrett and Co., *General and Commercial Directory of Burnley, Nelson, Colne and Padiham* (Barrett and Co., Preston: 1914).
27. Liddington, *Respectable Rebel*, pp. 67–9.
28. See Municipal Corporations Act, 1882 (45 & 46 Vict. c. 50); A. Lawrence Lowell, *The Government of England* (Macmillan and Co., London: 1908), ii, pp. 146–8.
29. *NL*, 10 January 1919.

Chapter 4

1. *Burnley Radical*, 8 January 1887.
2. See David Butler and Donald Stokes, *Political Change in Britain: Forces Shaping Electoral Choice* (Macmillan, London: 1969).
3. See Henry Pelling, *The Origins of the Labour Party 1880–1900* (Clarendon Press,

Oxford: 1965); Keith Laybourn, *The Rise of Labour: The British Labour Party 1890–1979* (Edward Arnold, London: 1988); 'The Rise of Labour and the Decline of Liberalism: The State of the Debate', *History* 80, 259 (1995), pp. 207–26.

4. P. F. Clarke, *Lancashire and the New Liberalism* (Cambridge University Press, Cambridge: 1971).

5. See Duncan Tanner, *Political Change and the Labour Party 1900–1918* (Cambridge University Press, Cambridge: 1990).

6. Philip Viscount Snowden, *An Autobiography* (Ivor Nicholson and Watson, London: 1934), i, p. 40.

7. *Blackburn Times*, 24 October 1885.

8. *NC*, 4 October 1890.

9. *Preston Guardian*, 31 October 1885.

10. *Burnley Radical*, 8 January 1887.

11. Anon., *The Origin and Progress of the Nelson Weavers' Association 1870–1920* (Burnley: 1922).

12. Nelson Weavers' Association (NWA), *Minute Book*, 25 July, 14 and 26 August 1890 (Lancashire County Record Office (CRO), DDX 1628: acc. 5856); Nelson and District Trades Council, *Minute Book*, 28 August 1890 (Lancashire CRO, DDX 1628: acc 5856); *NC*, 1 August, 26 September, 7 November 1890.

13. *Cotton Factory Times* (hereafter *CFT*), 31 October 1890.

14. See Roy Gregory, *The Miners and British Politics 1906–14* (Oxford University Press, Oxford: 1968).

15. See Jeffrey Hill, 'Social Democracy and the Labour Movement: the Social-Democratic Federation in Lancashire', *North West Labour History Society Bulletin* 8 (1982), pp. 44–55.

16. See David James, *Bradford* (Ryburn Publishing, Halifax: 1990), ch. 4.

17. See Jeffrey Hill, 'The ILP in Lancashire and the North West' in David James, Tony Jowitt and Keith Laybourn (eds), *The Centennial History of the Independent Labour Party* (Ryburn Academic Publishing, Halifax: 1992), pp. 43–62.

18. *CFT*, 15 December 1890.

19. NWA Minutes, 22 July 1891; 11 May, 24 September 1892; *CFT*, 24 June 1892.

20. *CFT*, 22 April 1892.

21. *NC*, 23 December 1892; *Burnley Socialist*, 28 October, 4 and 24 November 1893.

22. *NC*, 12 May 1893.

23. *Workman's Times*, 3 March 1894.

24. NWA Minutes, 13 January 1896.

25. See Pelling, *Origins*, ch. 10.

26. NWA, 12 July 1897; 10 July 1898; 30 August 1899; 15 July, 26 August, 23 September 1901.

27. *CFT*, 11 July 1902.

28. *Justice*, 5 April 1902.

29. *CFT*, 11 July 1902.

30. Clitheroe Division Labour Representation Association, rules set out in circular issued by national Labour Representation Committee, March 1902. (Labour Party Archives, *Infancy of Labour*, vol. i).

31. *CFT*, 6 October 1905.

32. 11 December 1903.

33. *CNT*, 3 November 1905; *NL*, 6 November 1903.

34. *NL*, 26 October, 2 and 9 November 1906; *CNT*, 29 October, 5 November 1909.

35. George I. Hawkes, *The Development of Public Education in Nelson* (Nelson Corporation, Nelson: 1966), pp. 167–76, 194–8.

36. See Ross McKibbin, *The Evolution of the Labour Party 1910–24* (Oxford University Press, Oxford: 1974), p. 19.

37. Karen Hunt, 'Women and the Social-Democratic Federation: Some Notes on Lancashire', *North West Labour History Society Bulletin* 7 (1980–81), pp. 49–64.

38. Jill Liddington, *The Life and Times of a Respectable Rebel: Selina Cooper (1864–1946)* (Virago, London: 1984), pp. 121–2.

39. Liddington, *Respectable Rebel*, pp. 176–7.

40. *NL*, 7 August 1914.

41. *The Leader War Record, 1914–15* (Coulton and Co. Ltd., Nelson: 1915), pp. 4, 23,

128 (Nelson Public Library). See also Peter Simkins, *Kitchener's Army: The Raising of the New Armies, 1914–16* (Manchester University Press, Manchester: 1988), pp. 52, 155.

42. *NL*, 18 December 1914.
43. See Roger Brown and Stan Iveson, *Clarion House: A Monument to a Movement* (Independent Labour Publications/Lancashire Polytechnic Community History Project, Preston: 1987), p. 23. The *Nelson Leader's* estimate for 1914 was 750, of which 250 were women (*NL*, 9 April 1914).
44. *NL*, 30 January 1914.
45. Arthur Marwick, *Clifford Allen: The Open Conspirator* (Oliver and Boyd, London: 1964), pp. 21–2; *NL*, 31 October 1914; Simkins, *Kitchener's Army*, p. 155.
46. Brown and Iveson, *Clarion House*, p. 36.
47. *NL*, 21 January, 3 March and 4 August 1916.
48. Liddington, *Respectable Rebel*, p. 276.
49. *NL*, 7 December 1917, 25 January, 8 February 1918, 24 December 1919.
50. *NL*, 3 January 1919.
51. *NL*, 7 November 1919, 5 November 1920.

Chapter 5

1. *Nelson and the Advantages it Offers for Industrial Enterprise* (Nelson Corporation, Nelson: 1919), p. 13.
2. See John Stevenson and Chris Cook, *Britain in the Depression: Society and Politics 1929–39* (Longman, Harlow: 1994).
3. J. B. Priestley, *English Journey* (Penguin Books, London: 1977), p. 375.
4. See Derek Beattie, *Blackburn: The Development of a Lancashire Cotton Town* (Ryburn Publishing, Halifax: 1992), ch. 9.
5. See e.g. Derek H. Aldcroft, *The Inter-War Economy: Britain 1919–39* (B. T. Batsford, London: 1970).
6. Lars G. Sandberg, *Lancashire in Decline: A Study in Entrepreneurship, Technology, and International Trade* (Ohio State University Press, Columbus, Ohio: 1974).
7. *NL*, 23 May 1930.
8. *NL*, 9 October 1914.
9. *NL*, 22 and 29 December 1922.
10. See Rex Pope, 'The Unemployment Problem in North East Lancashire, 1920–1938', M. Litt. thesis (University of Lancaster, 1974).
11. See *Ministry of Labour Gazette* (HMSO, London), vols xxxix (1931), xlii (1934), xliv (1936), xlvii (1939).
12. Pope, 'Unemployment Problem', p. 57.
13. *NL*, 27 December 1935.
14. Denise Martin, 'Women without Work: Textile Workers in North East Lancashire, 1919–39', MA thesis (University of Lancaster, 1985).
15. Barbara Drake and Margaret I. Cole (eds), *Beatrice Webb: Our Partnership* (Cambridge University Press, Cambridge: 1975), p. 24; Jeffrey Hill, 'Working Class Politics in Lancashire: A Study in the Regional Origins of the Labour Party, 1885–1906', Ph.D. thesis (University of Keele, 1969), pp. 50–5.
16. Alan Fowler, 'Trade Unions and Technical Change: The Automatic Loom Strike, 1908', *North West Labour History Society Bulletin* 6 (1978–80), pp. 43–55.
17. Nelson and District Manufacturers' Association (NDMA), *Minute Book*, 1930–32 (Lancashire CRO, DDX 1145, 3/1/13).
18. *NL*, 22 August 1930.
19. *NL*, 8 March 1935.
20. Full details in Alan and Lesley Fowler, *The History of the Nelson Weavers' Association* (Burnley, Nelson, Rossendale and District Textile Workers' Union, Nelson: n.d.), ch. 4.
21. Fowler, *Nelson Weavers*, p. 37.
22. Fowler, *Nelson Weavers*, p. 44.
23. Notes of General Council Meeting of the Amalgamated Weavers' Association, 21 July 1928 (Lancashire CRO, DDX 1123 6/2/279–86).

24. *NL*, 1 June 1928.
25. *NL*, 13 July 1928.
26. George Henry Wood, *The History of Wages in the Cotton Trade during the Past 100 Years* (Sherrattt and Hughes, London: 1910), p. 80.
27. Fowler, *Nelson Weavers*, pp. 64–5; Jill Liddington, *The Life and Times of a Respectable Rebel: Selina Cooper (1864–1946)* (Virago, London: 1984), pp. 389–93; Priscilla Ross, 'A Town Like Nelson: The Social Implications of Technical Change in a Lancashire Mill Town', Ph.D. thesis (University of Sussex, 1991), p. 121.
28. NDMA Minutes, 1930–2, 13 Jan. 1931.
29. *NL*, 8 May 1931.
30. NDMA Minutes, 1930–2, 7 July 1932.
31. NDMA Minutes, 1930–2, 1 June 1931.
32. NDMA Minutes, 1930–2, 10 June 1931.
33. *NL*, 15 May 1931.
34. *NL*, 8 May 1931.
35. Details from Aldcroft, *Inter-War Economy*, pp. 187–90; Douglas C. Hague, *The Economics of Man-Made Fibres* (Gerald Duckworth and Co., London: 1957), pp. 16–27.
36. *Nelsons of Nelson Ltd: The Story of James Nelson* (Harley Publishing Co., London: 1951); *NL*, 8 and 22 April 1927, 15 February 1929; *Lancashire Daily Post*, 18 May 1927.
37. W. Bennett, *The History of Marsden and Nelson* (Nelson Corporation, Nelson: 1957), p. 222; P. Barrett and Co., *General and Commercial Directory of Burnley, Nelson, Colne and Padiham* (Barrett and Co., Preston: 1940).
38. *Board of Trade Journal*, (HMSO London), 1 January 1945, pp. 406–7.

Chapter 6

1. Question said to have been put to a Nelson businessman by a government official, in the 1930s, quoted in Jill Liddington, *The Life and Times of a Respectable Rebel: Selina Cooper (1864–1946)* (Virago, London: 1984), p. 358. A good discussion of Nelson politics in the 1930s is to be found in Fiona Simpson, '"Moscow Calling": the Story of Radical Nelson', BA dissertation (University of Bradford, 1986).
2. *NL*, 4 and 6 May 1928, 23 May 1930.
3. Borough of Nelson, *Annual Report of the Medical Officer of Health and School Medical Officer for 1931* (Lancashire CRO, MBNe 16/1).
4. Borough of Nelson, *Municipal Year Book 1930–31* (Nelson Public Library); Borough of Nelson, *Nelson Corporation Jubilee, 1890–1940* (Nelson: 1946); *NL*, 24 January 1928, 19 June 1931.
5. *NL*, 22 November 1932.
6. Jane Mark-Lawson, 'Women, Welfare and Urban Politics: a Comparative Analysis of Luton and Nelson', Ph.D thesis (Lancaster University, 1987), p. 331.
7. John K. Walton, *Lancashire: A Social History 1558–1939* (Manchester University Press, Manchester: 1987), p. 311.
8. *NL*, 21 July 1922.
9. See *NL*, 2 June 1944.
10. Borough of Nelson, *Jubilee of the Incorporation of the Borough* (Coulton and Co., Nelson: 1946), p. 81.
11. See Jane Mark-Lawson, Mike Savage and Alan Warde, 'Gender and Local Politics: Struggles over Welfare Policies, 1918–39', in L. Murgatroyd (ed.), *Localities, Class and Gender* (Pion, London: 1985), pp. 195–217.
12. *NL*, 27 January 1922.
13. See below, Chapter 7, p. 111.
14. *NL*, 6 September 1932.
15. *Nelson Gazette (NG)*, 11 January 1938.
16. *NL*, 15 May 1931.
17. Details from 'Cotton Trade Dispute 1928' (CTD), file of miscellaneous letters and papers, Nelson Public Library; *NL*, 16 May, 4 November, 18 December 1931.
18. CTD, 1 and 28 June 1928.
19. CTD, 28 June 1928.

20. Liddington, *Respectable Rebel*, p. 351.
21. *NG*, 5 January, 6 September 1932.
22. *NL*, 24, 31 August, 16 November, 21 December 1934.
23. *NL*, 27 July 1930.
24. *NL*, 9 August 1935; *NG*, 11 January, 22 February 1938.
25. *New Leader*, 1 September, 17 November 1939.
26. *NL*, 4 April 1919.
27. See Liddington, *Respectable Rebel*, ch. 23.
28. *NL*, 22 December 1944.
29. *NL*, 9 April 1914.
30. Roger Brown and Stan Iveson, *Clarion House: A Monument to a Movement* (Independent Labour Publications/Lancashire Polytechnic Community History Project, Preston: 1987).
31. See below, Chapter 7, p. 110.
32. Brown and Iveson, *Clarion House*, p. 55.
33. *New Leader*, 1 September 1939.
34. See Duncan Tanner, *Political Change and the Labour Party, 1900–1918* (Cambridge University Press, Cambridge: 1990), pp. 143–4.
35. *Lancashire Daily Post*, 1 December 1910.
36. See Herbert Tracey (ed.), *The Book of the Labour Party*, vol. 2 (Caxton Publishing Co., London: n.d. [c.1925]), pp. 174–96.
37. Norman and Jeanne McKenzie (eds), *The Diary of Beatrice Webb, vol. 4, 1924–43* (Virago/London School of Economics, London: 1985), p. 431.
38. *NL*, 2 February 1934; Emrys Hughes, *Sydney Silverman: Rebel in Parliament* (Charles Skilton Ltd., London: 1969).
39. The Labour MP Judith Hart, elected to Parliament in 1959, regarded 'moderate' colleagues like Ben Parkin, Stephen Swingler, Harold Davies and George Wigg as being 'intelligent, thoughtful and not extreme back-benchers, who did not immediately go over the top on every issue, like Ian Mikardo or Sydney Silverman'; Ben Pimlott, *Harold Wilson* (Harper Collins, London: 1993), p. 237.
40. Details from *NL*, 4 and 11 November 1927; 26 October, 2 and 9 November 1934.

Chapter 7

1. *NL*, 8 August 1919.
2. *NL*, 21 March 1919. The *Leader* estimated that in the whole district (including Colne, Brierfield and Barrowford), the total figure for war deaths – as far as they had been notified to the paper – was 1,306.
3. Geoffrey Moorhouse, *Hell's Foundations: A Town, its Myths and Gallipoli* (Sceptre, London: 1993).
4. Moorhouse, *Hell's Foundations*, p. 200.
5. *NL*, 15 November 1918.
6. *NL*, 15 November 1918.
7. *NL*, 8 August 1919.
8. *NL*, 8 August 1919.
9. *NL*, 10, 17 January, 11 April 1919
10. See Vernon L. Lidtke, *The Alternative Culture: Socialist Labor in Imperial Germany* (Oxford University Press, Oxford: 1985); W. L. Guttsman, *The German Social Democratic Party: From Ghetto to Government, 1875–1933* (George Allen and Unwin, London: 1981).
11. Details from: *NG*, 3 January 1928; 4 January, 22 February 1938; Jill Liddington, *The Life and Times of a Respectable Rebel: Selina Cooper (1864–1946)*, (Virago, London: 1984), pp. 135–6.
12. *NG*, 10 and 24 January 1928, 8 March 1938.
13. *NG*, 28 May, 11 June 1929, 16 August 1932; *NL*, 5 December 1930.
14. *NG*, 13 March 1928; Priscilla Ross, 'A Town like Nelson: The Social Implications of Technical Change in a Lancashire Mill Town', D.Phil thesis (Sussex University, 1991), pp. 210–16.

15. *Official Handbook of the Stanley Street Methodist Church, 1886–1936* (Nelson: 1936) Nelson Public Library.
16. Temple Street Methodist Church, Nelson, *Jubilee Services 1896–1946* (Nelson: 1946) Nelson Public Library.
17. *NL*, 5 December 1930.
18. *NL*, 17 October 1930.
19. *NL*, 26 June 1931.
20. *NG*, 3 January 1928.
21. See *NL*, 18 August 1922.
22. *NG*, 14 May, 30 July, 31 December 1929, 5 January 1932, 2 August 1938.
23. It was less likely by the 1930s, for example, that an attendance as high as that at the Alma Grounds, Colne, in September 1911 could have been achieved when J. Howarth beat J. Lane by 20 yards with a stroke which measured 10 sc. 5 yards (*Colne and Nelson Times*, 15 September 1911). Nevertheless, knur and spell could still pull in big crowds; see Alan Tomlinson, 'Shifting Patterns of Working Class Leisure: The Case of Knur And Spell', *Sociology of Sport Journal* 9 (1992), pp. 192–206.
24. See *NL*, 1 May 1914; Robert Poole, *The Lancashire Wakes Holidays* (Lancashire County Books, Preston: 1994), p. 18 interestingly suggests the cock-fighting purpose. See also details in Henry Foulds, *A Selection of Newspaper Reports from Local Newspapers, 1875–1880*, p. 111 (Nelson Public Library).
25. *NG*, 20 March 1928.
26. *NL*, 8 June 1928, 17 October, 12 December 1930; 17 April, 19 June 1931.
27. C. E. Sutcliffe and F. Hargreaves, *History of the Lancashire Football Association, 1878–1928* (Yore Publications, Harefield, Middlesex: 1992), p. 211.
28. Details also from Dave Twydell, *Rejected FC*, vol. 1 (Yore Publications, Harefield, Middlesex: 1988), pp. 289–90.
29. Nelson Cricket and Bowling Club, *Secretary's Report*, 1924 (by kind permission of the Hon. Secretary, Nelson CC).
30. *NL*, 20 January 1922.
31. *Cricketer Annual, 1929–30* (*The Cricketer*, London), p. 66.
32. *NL*, 14 May 1937.
33. *NL*, 2 February 1934.
34. *NL*, 20 October 1936; *Gerald Howat, Learie Constantine* (George Allen and Unwin, London: 1975), pp. 79–80.
35. *NL*, 10 September 1937.
36. C. L. R. James, *Beyond a Boundary* (Stanley Paul, London: 1969), p. 127.
37. *NL*, 27 August 1937; see also Howat, *Learie Constantine*, pp. 97–8.
38. James, *Beyond a Boundary*, p. 110.
39. Colin Holmes, *John Bull's Island: Immigration and British Society* (Macmillan, London: 1988), pp. 202–3.
40. See *Sydney Daily Telegraph*, 9 July 1921.
41. See Jeffrey Hill, 'League Cricket in the North and Midlands', in Richard Holt (ed.), *Sport and the Working Class in Modern Britain* (Manchester University Press, Manchester: 1990), pp. 121–41; see also Jeffrey Hill, 'Cricket and the Imperial Connection: Overseas Players in Lancashire in the Inter-war Period', in John Bale and Joseph Maguire (eds), *The Global Sports Arena: Athletic Talent Migration in an Interdependent World* (Frank Cass, London: 1994), pp. 49–62.
42. *NG*, 9 April 1935.
43. *NG*, 9 April 1935. I am indebted to Evelyn O'Connor of the University of Central Lancashire for drawing my attention to this and the above reference.
44. *NL*, 17 January 1936.
45. *NL*, 6 June 1919.

Chapter 8

1. Lancashire County Council, *A Preliminary Plan for Lancashire (Interim Edition)* (Preston: 1950), p. 6.
2. *NL*, 28 December 1945.
3. *Nelsons of Nelson* (Harley Publishing Co., London: 1951), p. 46.

4. R. Robson, *The Cotton Industry in Britain* (Macmillan, London: 1957), especially pp. 13–18.

5. R. W. Lacey, 'Cotton's War Effort', *The Manchester School of Economic and Social Studies* 15 (1947), pp. 26–74.

6. Alan and Lesley Fowler, *The History of the Nelson Weavers' Association* (Burnley, Nelson,Rossendale and District Textile Workers' Union, Nelson: n.d.), p. 87.

7. *NG*, 29 September 1959.

8. Fowler, *Nelson Weavers*, p. 95

9. Quoted in Caroline Miles, *Lancashire Textiles: A Case Study of Institutional Change* (Cambridge University Press, Cambridge: 1968), p. 48.

10. *NG*, 18 May, 9 September 1959, 22 May 1962.

11. Robson, *Cotton Industry*, pp. 40, 44.

12. Quoted in Priscilla Ross, 'A Town like Nelson: The Social Implications of Technical Change in a Lancashire Mill Town' D.Phil thesis (Sussex University, 1991), p. 174. Permission to quote from this thesis has been sought by the author through Sussex University. Unfortunately, it was not possible to contact Dr Ross herself, and it is hoped that she will be agreeable to the use of short quotations from her work in this chapter.

13. Quoted in Ross, 'A Town like Nelson', pp. 174, 176.

14. *NG*, 29 September 1959.

15. Unemployment figures from Department of Employment, *Employment Gazette*, May 1970, February 1980, February 1985, April 1990; *Ministry of Labour Gazette*, vol. lxx (1962), p. 19; *Census of England and Wales ,1981, County Report: Lancashire* (London: 1982); *NL*, 30 January 1981.

16. Quoted in Ross, 'A Town like Nelson', p. 178.

17. Quoted in Ross, 'A Town like Nelson', p. 178.

18. *NG*, 4 October 1960.

19. T. W. Freeman, H. B. Rodgers and R. H. Kinvig, *Lancashire, Cheshire and the Isle of Man* (Nelson, London: 1966), p. 148.

20. *NG*, 21 July 1958.

21. *NL*, 28 June 1968.

22. *NL*, 30 January 1981.

23. See Lancashire County Council (County Planning Department), *Lancashire Structure Plan, 1991–2006 (Report 12: Economic Context)* (Preston: 1992).

24. Quoted in Ross, 'A Town like Nelson', p. 195.

25. Quoted in Ross, 'A Town like Nelson', p. 198.

26. For an interesting study of this whole issue, in the comparable Lancashire cotton town of Haslingden, see Geoffrey Pearson, ' "Paki-bashing" in a North East Lancashire Cotton Town: A Case Study and its History', in G. Mungham and G. Pearson, *Working Class Youth Culture* (Routledge Kegan and Paul, London: 1976), pp. 48–81.

27. Quoted in Ross, 'A Town like Nelson', p. 199.

28. Rolf Eriksson, *Survey of Ethnic Groups in Districts with Large Ethnic Population in the County of Lancashire* (Lancashire County Council, Preston: 1987), p. 97.

29. Eriksson, *Survey*, pp. 110–11.

30. Department of the Environment, *New Life in Old Towns: Report by Robert Matthew, Johnson-Marshall and Partners on Two Pilot Studies on Urban Renewal in Nelson and Rawtenstall Municipal Boroughs* (Department of the Environment, London: 1971), p. 13.

31. Figures on 'affluence' from *Census of England and Wales, 1961, 1971, 1981* (HMSO, London).

32. *The Guardian*, 18 June 1968.

33. *NL*, 21 June 1968; *The Guardian*, 26, 27 and 29 June 1968.

34. See Robert Waller, *The Almanac of British Politics*, 5th edn (Routledge, London: 1996), pp. 650–1.

35. Nikolaus Pevsner, *The Buildings of England: Lancashire 2, The Rural North* (Penguin Books, London: 1969), p. 180.

Index

List of subscribers

1. David Howorth, Nelson
2. Mr B. Cox, Foulridge
3. —
4. Jack Campy, Nelson
5. Paul Dale, Nelson
6. Len and Betty Dole, Nelson
7. —
8. Robert G. Jackson, Nelson
9. Ian L. Cox, Nelson
10. —
11. W. Edmondson, Roker, Sunderland
12. Evelyn O'Connor, Fulwood, Preston
13. Miss E. R. Flower, Fence, nr Burnley
14. Mrs Glenda Kenyon, Colne
15. Mrs P. J. Woodcock, Colne
16. J. Barry Fairhurst, Barrowford
17. Mr Graham Howard, Nelson
18. Mr P. S. Grindrod, Ontario, Canada
19. Colin Demaline, Brierfield
20. James Keith Starkie, Roughlee
21. Mr and Mrs G. Captsick, Nelson
22. —
23. Mr Frank Jackson, Barrowford
24. Mr and Mrs W. S. Jelley, Nelson
25. Joan Hudson, Barnoldswick
26. F. Kay Openshaw, Brierfield
27. Florence Openshaw, Brierfield
28. Peter W. Stanford, Greenfield, Colne
29. Christopher Allen, Nelson
30. Andrew Bracewell, Nelson
31. Gillian Chatterjee, Silver Springs, USA
32. Mrs Yvonne Marie Jackson, Nelson
33. Mr and Mrs Ian Metcalfe, Nelson
34. Barbara Sutcliffe, Nelson
35. Linda and Geoffrey Lord, Nelson
36. Brian Hill, Nelson
37. Carole Thursby, Barrowford
38. Mr Alan Webb, Nelson
39. Mrs P. Hayhurst, Nelson
40. Mrs Vivienne Marshall, Nelson
41. Mr D. Smales, Brierfield
42. Fred Sutcliffe, Nelson
43. June Thornber, Nelson
44. Mr and Mrs D. Hanson, Nelson
45. Mrs Dorothy Hartley, Brierfield
46. Miss D. A. Walton, Brierfield
47. Mr and Mrs A. Brown, Burnley
48. Mr and Mrs W. Walton, Brierfield
49. Frank and Hilary Coyne, Nelson
50. —
51. Joan Snowden, Colne
52. Howard Nutter, Trawden
53. Mrs J. Ashworth, Brierfield
54. Mr W. Eccles, Brierfield
55. Jack Day, Nelson
56. —
57. Michael J. Morris, Nelson
58. Mr D. Hutchinson, Barrowford
59. Mrs Spencer, Nelson
60. Richard Gibson Knowles, Nelson
61. Norman and Audrey Ambler, Brierfield
62. Mrs Iris Wareing, Nelson
63. —
64. E. I. Reynard, Nelson
65. Mr Anthony Hughes, Nelson
66. —
67. Mrs M. Akrigg, Brierfield
68. P. and K. Dorrington, Brierfield
69. Mr John Gordon Ingham, Nelson
70. Margery and Eddie Plant, Nelson
71. —
72. Fred and Carole Nutter, Barrowford
73. Mrs J. Greenwood, Colne
74. Paul Gribble, Nelson
75. S. Barnes, Nelson
76. Mr I. M. Ingham, Nelson
77. Harold and Noella Duxbury, Nelson
78. Bob Gordon, Nelson
79. Mrs M. Edmondson, Nelson
80. Mr Peter Harris, Nelson

81. Mr H. Hobman, Nelson
82. Mr Len Short, Tasmania
83. Mr L. D. Pollard, Nelson
84. —
85. M. and T. Blackburn, Nelson
86. Mr David Brookes and Mrs Sandra Brooks, Colne
87. Mr Frank Bardgett and Mrs Grace Bardgett, Nelson
88. Mr Jonathan Ramsden Barrett, Nelson
89. Mrs Kathleen Haydock, Salterforth, Barnoldswick
90. Mr M. Stobbs, Nelson
91. Donald James Smith, Nelson
92. Mr Thomas A. Cooper, Brierfield
93. R. and B. Standage, Nelson
94. Mr John Burgoyne, Barrowford
95. Mr and Mrs B. Boden, Nelson
96. Mr B. A. Cosgrove, Nelson
97. Mr and Mrs B. L. Askew, Rosegrove, Burnley
98. W. Smith, Brierfield
99. Mr F. Melling, Barrowford
100. Miss Amanda Westwell, Colne
101. Susan Cooper, Nelson
102. Graham Stone, Twyford, Berks
103. Denis Flory, Roughlee
104. Pamela J. White, Barrowford
105. Jean-Gordon Thorpe, Nelson
106. Mrs Phyllis J. Counsell, Nelson
107. Mrs A. Burrows, Nelson
108. Mr and Mrs D. Kitson, Nelson
109. Mrs D. Shapland, Nelson
110. Mrs Anne Riley, Barrowford
111. Mr B. Clegg, Nelson
112. Mrs K. Taylor, Higherford, Nelson
113. Susan Sparks, Nelson
114. Mr Paul Martin, Nelson
115. Elsie Judson, Nelson
116. —
117. Hazel Barnes, Higherford, Nelson
118. Mrs Hannah Gates, Nelson
119. Mr Donald L. Short, Nelson
120. Mr Harry Rycroft, Nelson
121. Philip J. Haythornthwaite, Barrowford
122. Sylvia and Kenneth Hirst, Barrowford
123. Mr Stephen G. Hirst, Barrowford
124. Mr Philip K. Hirst, Barrowford
125. Mr Andrew J. Hirst, Barrowford
126. Mr R. F. Watts, Nelson
127. Councillor Roger Abbiss, Barrowford
128. Mrs Doreen Gallagher, Nelson
129. Mr Norman Halstead, New Zealand
130. Mrs S. Howarth, Colne
131. Mrs Jean E. Swain, Fence, Burnley
132. Mrs Norma Dower, Colne
133. Francis Thornton, Nelson
134. Mr Frank Edmondson, Nelson
135. Mr J. Burrows, Brierfield
136. Wilfred Foster, Nelson
137. Mr Danny McNamara, Nelson
138. Gwen Lees, Burnley
139. Mrs Pearl Kendall, Colne
140. —
141. Mrs Joan Knapp, Rimington, Clitheroe
142. A. H. Properties, Nelson
143. Joan Hobson, Nelson
144. H. K. Groves, Barrowford
145. Arnold Foulds Lindsay, Foulridge
146. Alan Stuttard, Fence, Burnley
147. Mr Anthony Robinson, Nelson
148. John Cockshott, Nelson
149. M. and A. Campbell, Nelson
150. Denis Lovell, Nelson
151. Mr Geoffrey and Mrs Ruth Sutton, Foulridge
152. Trevor Walsh, Nelson
153. Graham Altham-Lewis, Nelson
154. K. J. Hartley, Barrowford
155. J. Green, Nelson
156. —
157. —
158. Mrs Jacqui King, Trawden
159. Mr M. R. and Mrs A. P. Bury, Barrowford
160. Richard Mellor, Fence, Burnley
161. Stephen T. Bannister, Nelson
162. Victor Edwin Ainsworth, Nelson
163. Mr Bernard Tansey, Nelson
164. Mr B. Fitzpatrick, Nelson
165. Keith and Doreen Walmsley, Nelson
166. Mr T. Procter, Colne
167. Empress Mill (1927) Ltd, Colne
168. R. J. Hayhurst, Barley
169. Mildred Iris Emma Alderson (née Greenbank), Nelson
170. Mr David Robertson, Trawden
171. Mr M. Robinson, Barrowford
172. Mr and Mrs H. Gregg, Nelson
173. J. R. Burrows, Nelson

174. Adam Metcalfe, Barley
175. Mr and Mrs M. C. Greenwood, Nelson
176. J. N. Hitchen, Burnley
177. J. and M. Burgess, Barrowford
178. Keith Ingham, Nelson
179. Kenneth Baldwin, Melbourne, Australia
180. Mr and Mrs L. Stobbs, Nelson
181. Joan Shackleton, Nelson
182. Marjorie Hargreaves, Waddington
183. R. L. Cockerill, Brierfield
184. Jean Hartley, Burnley
185. Frank Chadwick, Nelson
186. Mr R. N. Morris, Nelson
187. A. M. and H. Hartley, Brierfield
188. Graham F. Carter, Nelson
189. Brenda Hillman, Nelson
190. Edward Sutcliffe, Fence, Burnley
191. Derrick A. Potter, Nelson
192. Mr D. Leeming, Brierfield
193. William Holden, Nelson
194. Gareth John Slater, Nelson
195. Pendle Village Mill, Brierfield
196. Mr Sydney Lingard, Nelson
197. Mrs A. Rogers, Nelson
198. Mr A. E. Hughes, Fence, Burnley
199. Mrs M. Duerden, Burnley
200. Robert Anderson, Nelson
201. M RR. J. Devanney, Burnley
202. Jack and Madelene Manley, Nelson
203. Christopher Clark, Brierfield
204. Lynda Melville, Nelson
205. Mr M. J. Brett, Nelson
206. Mrs M. R. Threadgill, Colne
207. Steven John Bury, Nelson
208. Mrs M. Sourbutts, Nelson
209. Sylvia Rayson, Colne
210. Mrs M. Porter, Nelson
211. Kevin R. Whiteley, Barrowford
212. Landon Bolton, Colne
213. Mr R. Percival, Colne
214. Elaine Hoggarth, Colne
215. Mr P. F. Bebington, Nelson
216. —
217. Carol Carr Billington, Warton, Preston
218. Mr E. Midgley, Barrowford
219. —
220. Mrs June Leeper, Nelson
221. Ian S. McInery, Sabden
222. Edmund Lee, Nelson
223. Peter Robert Riley, Colne
224. Mrs Maureen Tipping, Nelson

225. —
226. Mrs B. Jackson, Nelson
227. —
228. Mr A. Shuttleworth, Nelson
229. Mr Simon C. Lucas, Reedley, Burnley
230. Roy Hughes, Nelson
231. Tom Hargreaves, Brierfield
232. Mrs Elsie Broughton, Nelson
233. Mr Albert H. Savage, Nelson
234. Mr Brian Spencer, Colne
235. Mrs Mary Lancaster, Brierfield
236. Edna Wood, Nelson
237. Harry Pinder, Nelson
238. Mrs R. G. Winter, Colne
239. Kenneth Deighton, Nelson
240. John and Sylvia Clayton, Barrowford
241. —
242. Geoffrey Yates, Brierfield
243. David Hird, Warrington
244. —
245. Mrs O. Burton, Nelson
246. Mrs Vera Watson, Brierfield
247. Mr William Wells, Colne
248. Mr Stuart M. Hall, Colne
249. Mr D. Storton, Brierfield
250. Mrs Irene Westell, Trawden
251. Mr T. D. Windle, Barrowford
252. Christine Ryan, Nelson
253. H. Wilkinson, Nelson
254. Norman S. Carter, Nelson
255. J. M. and A. Stacey, Roughlee
256. Mrs Jennifer Petty, Foulridge
257. Janet E. Payton, Colne
258. Alec W. Holt, Blacko
259. Mr Lawrence Mutter, Nelson
260. Mr Ronnie Williamson, Roughlee
261. Tracey Sanderson, Burnley
262. Linda Pearson, Barnoldswick
263. Jack Gray and Kathleen Gray, Barrowford
264. Mr Ronald A. Sugden, Salterforth
265. Pat and Peter Atkinson, Nelson
266. Mr G. Bentley, Nelson
267. —
268. Edward M. Ellis, Brierfield
269. Learning Resource Centre, Nelson & Colne College
270. Mr F. Barrett, Foulridge
271. Mr Frererick Wilcock, Nelson
272. Mrs Eunice Belshaw, Brierfield
273. Mr and Mrs R. Palmer, Reedley Hallows

274. Mrs Shirley Ingham, Brierfield
275. Derek Pickles, Cliviger
276. Mrs and Mrs J. Richardson, Rotorua, New Zealand
277. Andrew J. E. Duerden, Nelson
278. Mrs Anne Clancy JP, Nelson
279. Mrs Mary Selby, Wolverton, Milton Keynes
280. Anthony B. Helmn, Nelson
281. Mr Norris Edmondson, Nelson
282. Mr B. R. Thomason, Nelson
283. Ian Murgatroyd, Nelson
284. Ian Forrester, Nelson
285. Mr Brian Dickinson, Nelson
286. Norman Cowgill, Winewall, Colne
287. Norman J. Ayre, Nelson
288. Mr Peter Cichocki, Nelson
289. Mrs Dorothea Wardell, Nelson
290. George Henry Davies, Barrowford
291. Mrs June Proudfoot, Trawden
292. Mrs L. Midgley, Foulridge
293. Mr Geoffrey Boothman, Corsham
294. —
295. P. S. Walsh, Nelson
296. Allan and Dorothy MacInnes, Nelson
297. Peter Dewhurst, Nelson
298. Sister Mary Wereburga (Catherine Hargrave)
299. Miss Doris Monk, Nelson
300. Mr Stanley Phillips, Nelson
301. Mrs Christine Betts, Nelson
302. Frank Cooke, Colne
303. Victoria Cooke, Colne
304. David Tonks, Hertford
305. Pauline Davies, Foulridge
306. Mrs S. Curbelo, Barrowford
307. Glenys Barnes, Nelson
308. Mr Carl Short, Nelson
309. —
310. —
311. —
312. Albert and Barbara Milligan, Reedley Hallows
313. —
314. Mr A. Brown, Nelson
315. Mr Stephen Green, Nelson
316. Mr P. Furness, Nelson
317. J. and J. W. Hudson, Nelson
318. —
319. Mr Alan Bailey, Nelson
320. June and James Knowles, Nelson
321. Norma Bowes, Trawden
322. Mrs E. J. Timberlake, Barrowford

323. Trevor M. Smith, Nelson
324. John and Noreen Wilson, Ulverston
325. Mr Jack Brown, Nelson
326. John Warburton, Burnley
327. K. and S. M. Rycroft, Nelson
328. Mr P. G. and Mrs J. Sisterson, Nelson
329. Mr H. W. Johnson, Nelson
330. Mrs Pamela O'Conner, Colne
331. D. E. and D. K. Roper, Nelson
332. Mrs S. Cooks, Barrowford
333. Mrs Edna Whittaker, Nelson
334. Vicky Neal, Nelson
335. Mrs M. Porter, Nelson
336. Dorothy Denton, Colne
337. Mr and Mrs W. Walton, Brierfield
338. Mrs Y. Leaver, Barrowford
339. Mrs Gwendoline Mary Hodkinson, Nelson
340. Gordon Heap, Nelson
341. Mrs P. Bannister, Barrowford
342. Michael Pettitt, Sheffield
343. F. and E. Hindle, Nelson
344. Christine Ann Moore, Whitecross, Cornwall
345. Mr Graham Richard Pickles, Nelson
346. Peter Boothman, Nelson
347. Joe Winkley, Nelson
348. Simon Winkley, Nelson
349. Sarah Winkley, Nelson
350. William Townson Demain, Colne
351. David J. Horth, Arndale Shopping Centre, Nelson
352. Mr Sidney A. Dale, Barrowford
353. Harry C. Manning, Barrowford
354. John Cooper, Nelson
355. Neville Crowson, Colne
356. Margaret Mary Jennings, Nelson
357. Nora Foster, Nelson
358. Mrs Margaret Arnold M.B.E., Brierfield
359. Mr A. Watson, Nelson
360. Mrs Jean Whittaker, Brierfield
361. Mary Murthwaite, Colne
362. Mr Michael Anthony Stables, Nelson
363. Mrs J. Heaton, Nelson
364. Mrs Florence Bussy, Nelson
365. Mr and Mrs R. Yates, Nelson
366. Mrs Irene Lias, Nelson
367. James A. Waddington, Nelson
368. Fred Coates, Nelson

369. J. and A. M. Barrowclough, Nelson
370. J. B. Hoyle, Arnside
371. Mrs Janet O'Connor, Hinckley
372. Mr Barry Jackson, Roughlee
373. Mr A. E. Howorth, Nelson
374. Keith and Dianne Rumfitt, Nelson
375. James and Susan Rumfitt, Nelson
376. John, Victoria and Rebecca Davies, Southampton
377. Betty North, Canada
378. D. K. Scott, Nelson
379. H. Aughton, Berkhamstead
380. Peter Moorby Reed, Skipton
381. —
382. Mrs M. Smith, Nelson
383. Christopher George Murray, Brierfield
384. Mr Alan Fox, Nelson
385. Ivy Chadwick, Nelson
386. Mr and Mrs T. Dicken, Nelson
387. Colin Stuart Cowgill, Nelson
388. Barry Smithson, Nelson
389. Mr G. Newsham, Brierfield
390. Peter Maxwell Catlow, Nelson
391. Roger Meadowcroft, Darwen
392. Alan Rodwell, Nelson
393. Mr J. Moore, Nelson
394. Stephen Owen, Nelson
395. Dennis Hogarth, Gloucester
396. Mr. J Ingerton, Nelson
397. Mrs S. Robinson, Barrowford
398. Mrs Susan Lister, Nelson
399. Mrs J. Spencer, Nelson
400. Derek John Bailey, Nelson
401. Mr George Lee, Higherford
402. Mrs Joan Ford, Burnley
403. Mrs Rona Porter, Barrowford
404. Mrs Janet Chadwick, Barrowford
405. Mrs Blackburn, Nelson
406. Robert Tillotson, Barrowford
407. Mrs Margaret Parker, Brierfield
408. J. W. and R. I. Proctor, Nelson
409. Mrs Susan Byrne, Nelson
410. —
411. Mr and Mrs F. Proctor, Brierfield
412. Mr A. Lawson, Burnley
413. Malcolm C. Sterratt, Barnoldswick
414. Jennifer Jamieson, Colne
415. Mr and Mrs J. K. Smith, Burnley
416. Mr and Mrs Robert Atkinson, Burnley
417. Bernard and Pauline Oldham, Nelson
418. James Sanderson, Barrowford
419. Mr and Mrs Ronald Hunt, Burnley
420. —
421. Mr Wilfred L. Newman, Nelson
422. Mrs Sheila M. Markendale, Colne
423. Margaret Irza, Nelson
424. Mrs J. M. Bridge, Nelson
425. Mr F. Hothersall, Burnley
426. Mrs E. Titherington, Colne
427. H. Charlett, Nelson
428. —
429. Mrs Nancy Barton, Nelson
430. —
431. —
432. —
433. —
434. Kathleen Marie Ashworth, Nelson
435. John H. Farrow, Burnley
436. Mr Francis Morrison, Colne
437. Mr and Mrs John Greenwood, Barrowford
438. Constance and Doreen Metcalfe, Colne
439. Mrs Gail Firmin, Nelson
440. Guy Jefferson, Nelson
441. Stanley John Fincham, Barrowford
442. Mr Jack Bowell, Nelson
443. Lorraine McFadyen, Colne
444. Mr Ian J. Williams, Brierfield
445. Mr Colin Bell, Brierfield
446. Mr G. Bancroft, Nelson
447. R. J. Irving, Nelson
448. Herbert Sagar, Burnley
449,
450. Mrs L. Duxbury, Barrowford
451. Ian George Pendlebury, Brierfield
452. Moira Parkington, Nelson
453. Mr C. G. Akrill, Nelson
454. —
455. Paul Morris, Colne
456. Derick Harrison, Colne
457. Mr J. D. Catlow, Brierfield
458. Mr and Mrs D. Richardson, Colne
459. Margaret Lupton, Barrowford
460. Victor Lupton, Barrowford
461. Mr Keith Swarbrick
462. Ralph Latham, Colne
463. Mr Rodney Blezard, Nelson
464. Mr William Barrington Higgin, Nelson
465. Derek and Dot Procter, Nelson
466. Marsden County Primary School, Nelson
467. Colne and District Local History Society